Zen Gardening

Zen Gardening

A. K. Davidson

RIDER
London Melbourne Sydney Auckland Johannesburg

Rider and Company

An imprint of the Hutchinson Publishing Group

17–21 Conway Street, London W1P 6JD

Hutchinson Group (Australia) Pty Ltd
30–32 Cremorne Street, Richmond South, Victoria 3121
PO Box 151, Broadway, New South Wales 2007

Hutchinson Group (NZ) Ltd
32–34 View Road, PO Box 40-086, Glenfield, Auckland 10

Hutchinson Group (SA) Pty Ltd
PO Box 337, Bergvlei 2012, South Africa

First published 1982
© A. K. Davidson 1982

Set in Linotron Bembo by
A-Line Services, Saffron Walden, Essex

British Library Cataloguing in Publication Data
Davidson, A. K.
 Zen gardening.
 1. Gardening 2. Zen Buddhism
 I. Title
 635   SB454

ISBN 0 09 146301 7

MIX
Paper from
responsible sources
FSC® C018072

Printed and bound in Great Britain by Clays Ltd, St Ives PLC

For Yvonne, with thanks

Contents

Acknowledgements

I have been greatly indebted to a number of people while writing this book, and would like to thank them, and the many others who offered advice now and then, for their help and guidance. In Japan I must particularly thank Ichiro Harada, Noboru Hitani, M. Miyamoto and Fusa Kondo for what they have taught me and without whose general assistance the book could not have been written. In England, for their support and help while I was preparing the manuscript, I must thank Basil and Marion Davidson, Kyron and Lyn Lawford, and, finally, Mary McGuinness who typed it all up for me.

Introduction

It is difficult when discussing any aspect of Japanese culture clearly to define origins, influences or stages of development. In talking about Japan we are dealing with a nation, its culture, religions and senses of aesthetics, which until this century has been almost entirely isolated and growing within itself. The products of crafts, the artifacts, the buildings and the gardens that can be seen in modern Japan are the most recent developments in a long line of artistic concepts that stretches back unbroken for over a thousand years. It is this depth of tradition and its importance to the Japanese, that has enabled their culture to hold its own against the upheavals of the present century, and to still be a dynamic, living part of Japanese life.

In this way the concept of gardening in Japan, although some of the gardens are now very old and serve mainly as tourist attractions, is still very much a living one, with traditional ideas being used throughout the country to create gardens of all sizes. In saying this I hope to make it clear that the idea behind using these techniques today is not one of re-creating something lost, or of following long-out-of-date rules, but of using them for a new approach to natural elements in garden design. This approach has not only the feel of history, timeless and tried, but can also suggest a wealth of new ideas for making more of the space available.

Without doubt, one of the major factors behind Japan's historical cultural cohesion and its continuing strength today has been the influence of Zen Buddhism. After its arrival in Japan around 1200 A.D., Zen rapidly combined with, or superseded, the existing philosophical and religious systems to become the driving force behind almost every aspect of cultural and aesthetic development. It is a measure of the unique position Zen Buddhism occupies in Japan that this book should be called *Zen Gardening*, because although, as

11

we shall see, there are other influences present in the history of Japanese gardens, all of which contributed something in terms of concept and designs, it was the introduction of Zen and the work of the Zen priest-gardeners, that really moulded the ideas and techniques into a 'way of gardening' that is still practised in Japan, hundreds of years later, and has attracted the attention and admiration of people throughout the world.

In this book, therefore, I have attempted to explain the relationship between Zen and the development of gardens and then to look at the details of design and construction against this background. One thought to bear in mind while reading the book is that at the heart of Zen lies the concept of the 'Way' – the road that must be taken to achieve understanding. Above I have used the phrase 'way of gardening', taken from the title of a medieval Japanese book on gardening techniques, and it should be noted that the word 'way' here is used as much in the Zen sense, as to explain methods or techniques; for the concepts of 'Japanese gardening' and 'Zen gardening' are to all intents and purposes the same.

A.K.D.
September 1981

1

Zen and the Gardens

The key to the Buddhist mysteries lies in what passed through the Buddha's mind as he sat alone, talking to no one and reading no books, determined to achieve understanding even if he died in the attempt. After several days, sitting in the same spot, totally still, he gained his 'enlightenment'; by a process of meditation over an extended period he had realized the truth of how things really are, the realities of 'being', and it remained now to pass on to others the way in which this enlightenment may be achieved.

After Buddha's death his disciples decided that this should be done by collecting together his sayings and the tales of his actions so that the resulting scriptures (known now as the *Pali Canon*) could be studied as the way to achieving enlightenment. It was not long, however, before disputes arose about the *Pali Canon* between followers of Buddhism, and from these there developed a number of schools of thought, who differed in their view of the *Canon's* wording, order and, perhaps most important, its role in the teaching of Buddhism. The most direct challenge to the traditional view, which maintained that studying and learning the scriptures was essential to understanding, came from the school which held that, on the contrary, meditation (Dhyana), the process by which the Buddha achieved enlightenment, was the key to realization of the truth. The Dhyana school grew steadily in India and was eventually brought to China by the monk Bodhidharma during the sixth century A.D., where it became known as the Ch'an sect. After becoming totally assimilated with the Chinese culture and concepts of philosophical thought, Ch'an (pronounced Zen in Japanese) spread first to Korea and then, during the twelfth century, to Japan.

The impact of this meditative approach to Buddhism on Japan was immediate and this can be seen not least in the dramatic changes

13

evident in the development of gardening. Before looking at these, however, we might look quickly at those aspects of Zen thought which had a bearing on those changes. Basically the ideas of the Dhyana school, after being refined by Bodhidharma and subsequent masters, revolved around the actual beginning of Buddhism, the moment of Buddha's enlightenment. The truths he discovered were already there within him but had previously been too deeply hidden by confusion and illusion to be perceived. So the Zen masters concentrated on techniques of 'seeing' through the illusions and sorting out the confusion, as a way to discovering the truths of how and what things really are. In this way, Zen is a process by which man recognizes what he actually is. Most important in this for us is that this idea of transmitting the truth relied not on teachings and written scriptures, but on the sudden flashes of insight that can be triggered in a state of meditation, by a single word, an action, a noise or even an arrangement of rocks It is the job, therefore, of the Zen master to provide suitable stimulation to individual students at appropriate moments during training, to help guide them towards understanding, rather than by conventional methods of teaching. Whether he does this by a word, an action or choosing a particular place for meditation depends on the particular student, but all the time his aim is to help them along the way to understanding.

As important as any of the techniques the masters used to aid enlightenment were those that used visual stimulation. Of these some involved actions and some contemplation of an object or objects, and included in the latter category were the gardens that were set up in and around Zen monasteries. Through this connection and, as we shall see, others that grew up with it, Zen soon occupied a central position in Japanese culture, affecting every aspect of it from that day to this.

The reasons why the Zen sect became so rapidly and deeply absorbed into Japanese society will, I hope, become clear when we look at the historical development of gardens in Japan during which the impact of Zen is immediately noticeable, but before going on to this I should like to put things into some kind of geographical context. The importance of this is that the physical characteristics of Japan, not always fully appreciated by outsiders, have had a considerable bearing on the kind of garden that developed, even if philosophical and religious thought have provided the actual ideas and details. Japan is first and foremost a land dominated by mountains. An unbroken chain of mountains runs right down the largest island, Honshu, gathering in the centre to form the massive bulk of the Japanese Alps. The mountain peaks here rise to 10,000 and 11,000 feet; sharp, steep-sided ridges join them and the slopes are covered with trees and dense undergrowth. The inaccessibility of these mountain ranges and the lack of wide valleys between them, mean that the people of Japan live on the crowded coastal plains and in the valleys of large rivers. Indeed, it is a celebrated fact that some seventy or eighty per cent of the nation live on just three per cent of the land. The importance of this geography for our purposes lies in three areas.

The first of these is concerned with the atmosphere that these mountains create with their steep, inaccessible peaks and ridges rising into mists and clouds; the deep vegetation and towering trees; jagged outcrops, boulders, and ravines alive with tumbling water. The forests and mountains were, and in some cases still are, home for wild boar, wolves, wildcats, hawks and kites. With the ferocious thunderstorms and typhoons of autumn and the deep snows of winter, active volcanoes and boiling mineral springs, this was the realm of nature. The mountains dominate the routes of communication between the towns nestled in them and are an ever-present part of life. All this gives them an importance and a role in Japanese life that should not be ignored. The air of mystery that surrounds them, which is similar to that represented in the old *sansui* pen and ink paintings from China, leads to a meditative approach that contrasts with the more practical Western approach to the more accessible, rolling and usable hills of Europe and much of America.

This leads to our second point which is that as a result of the above, the Japanese have traditionally preferred looking at mountains rather than climbing or being amongst them. The contemporary popularity of climbing, mountain walking, hiking and skiing does not really alter this cultural tradition. Rather than scenery, as a whole the Japanese have tended to prefer looking at a particular scene, whether this be the view through a window, the work of an artist's imagination or the re-creation of natural scenes in the form of a garden. This too may be an indication of the influence of the scroll paintings which were generally imaginary landscapes based on the physical characteristics of the Chinese mainland, Korea and later Japan, instead of reproductions of actual views. The important elements were grouped together to represent the landscape.

Having noted this we come to the third point. Then, as now, because of geographical restrictions Japanese society was very centralized, concentrated in the few areas suitable for the growth of large cities. This had two effects of interest to us. First it meant that new ideas, once established in the courts of the emperors, military lords or religious leaders, the people of influence, they spread very rapidly along the few routes of communication to all other large centres of population, most of which are sprawled across the southern shores of Honshu. So it was with Zen Buddhism, which soon established itself in the major military, religious and social centres. The second point is that the social and administrative centres soon grew into the crowded, teeming towns and cities for which Japan is famous today, where very few houses have what Westerners would term a 'garden' due to the lack of space. So, in the small areas and yards around the houses, the Japanese preference for small 'scenes' and the meditative approach of Zen Buddhism, combined effortlessly to produce small landscaped 'gardens' that could offer some relief and peace of mind to counter the effects of high-density living and bring into the urban surroundings something of the moun-tains and their spaces and serenity. Gardens were symbolic of this greater outside; people could contemplate them and regain some perspective on life; they could enter a different mood for a while, depending on the kind of miniaturized scene they chose to construct.

From the above background it can be seen that Japan was in many ways ideally suited to the ideas of Zen. The new form of Buddhism fitted the meditative, philosophical nature of the Japanese and their environment. Let's look now at how the arrival of Zen revolution-ized the development of the gardens, and start by going back to the very beginnings of Japanese landscape art.

I mentioned in the Introduction that defining the origins of Japanese culture is at best difficult, and gardens are no exception. A garden in Japan can be anything from a small corner containing a stone lantern and a rock, to a large area including ponds and waterfalls.

Impressions can be just as varied: a bowl set amongst dense foliage, a stone path beside a pool, piled rocks flanking a tumbling waterfall, a pine tree arching out over a stream; a wealth of detail seen or suggested almost dreamlike amongst delicate maple leaves that sway and catch the sun. Or wide sweeps of white gravel flowing around groups of stones and miniature trees, a background of rocks or a pond stretching away, full of islands and fish. On their own or in combination, these impressions represent the basic elements that

16

make up the gardens and it is in the use of gravel and rocks that we find the first clues as to how the Japanese garden developed.

Before the introduction of Buddhism into Japan around 600 A.D., the native beliefs, loosely grouped under the name Shinto, were based on the worship of natural phenomena and the ancestors. The part of this which interests us concerns the worship of natural phenomena that were outstanding in some way – in shape or size, beauty, or age, anything indeed that set the particular object apart from others. Thus the object of worship could be a mountain, like Mt Fuji which is set apart by its almost perfect conical shape, or a particularly old tree, a large rock, or a smaller but pleasingly shaped rock. Similarly, particular waterfalls or springs were worshipped. The people were appealing to the spirits that resided within the object for good health, long life, good harvests, good luck and so on. Due to its special qualities the object became sacred and this included the area immediately around it.

Once a particular object or place had come to be worshipped then the area immediately around it became sacred and was marked off with either a ring of stones or ropes. The size of the area depended on the importance of the spirits and could be a few square feet or, in the case of the national shrines, several acres and even whole mountains. Once the area was marked off no one, except priests, leaders or emperors, could enter, since any other presence would destroy the purity of the place.

Since these ancient beliefs were primarily aimed at ensuring good health, removal of disease, or cleansing of thought and body, purity and purifying was of prime importance. Thus these centres of worship were basically centres purified for worship, and to approach and benefit from the spirits the worshipper must also be purified. The crucial purifying agent was water and it was for this reason that water was inevitably present at these places in some form or another. Maybe a waterfall or stream, or if not naturally present, in water-bowls for hand washing and mouth rinsing. The area would be cleared and often spread with gravel or small stones, the sound of which, when walked on, helped the worshipper to enter a calmer, more removed state of mind. The area would often be completed by the planting of a sacred Sasaki tree, symbolizing the ancient creators of the country.

The similarities between the components of these old sites and those of the subsequent gardens are pretty clear and give us a start in tracing the origins of the gardens. Further evidence of this link between the two is that one of the first words used to indicate a garden and which carries the same meaning now, was *niwa*, which literally meant 'pure place'. In addition to these points the importance of the sun goddess (Amaterasu-o-no-kami) as the central figure in the pantheon of gods is reflected in the general orientation of gardens. As a guiding rule the traditional gardens of Japan were laid out on an east/west arrangement, facing south, so that artificial lakes and streams, when viewed from the north, would run left to right. The garden thus became a rough representation of the sun's course, following the direction and flow of the life-giving source.

The other main area in which the early shrines influenced the development of gardens were the larger spaces set aside for the worship of a variety of spirits. These places were almost parks in which people strolled along laid-out paths passing from one roped-off group to another. The various points of worship, which later developed into elements for gardens were thus joined together to create a much larger whole. They were joined for the people by paths, and in 'spirit' by the great purifier, water, which flowing from a sacred spring would be fed down waterfalls to fill large ponds, passing as it went a number of other sacred points such as trees or rocks. This unification reflected the great oneness of nature and created 'pure' places on a large scale. Later, of course, the water courses and paths developed design principles of their own and became important garden elements in their own right.

From the above we can discern some of the starting places of design and content concepts that later became integral in garden construction. Here are the origins of focusing the attention on groups and the idea of passing from one group to another, which are fundamental parts of Japanese garden design. In addition we have the origins of the idea of roping areas off, which leads directly to the concept of looking at and contemplating the area rather than entering and using it. Over and above these more direct points the design principles of Shinto shrines exerted an immediate influence on the gardens that were based on later imported Chinese models and on temple gardens that were created after the introduction of Buddhism from the mainland. In this way these early ideas contributed to the alteration of imported ideas and led to the development of a distinct Japanese garden.

The years around 600 A.D. saw unprecedented activity between Japan and the mainland – trade, travel and the passing of ideas between the courts of the Japanese emperors and those of the Korean and Chinese kings. Among the more important of these exchanges was the introduction into Japan from China via Korea of Buddhism. Thus the Japanese received Buddhist ideas that had been influenced, redirected and modified by the art and aesthetic and religious concepts of the great Chinese civilization. The Chinese, and subsequently the Korean kingdoms, instead of adopting all the iconography and religious arts of India, had developed their own ways of expressing and representing the great truths of Buddhism. It was these techniques, subtly influenced by the older existing ideas we have looked at above, that led to the development of the garden in Japan.

Once the Buddhist faith had begun to find acceptance amongst the Japanese, craftsmen and builders were brought over to Japan to help build suitable temples and grounds wherein the new Buddhist deities could be worshipped. Thus in 618 the first-known garden, that is to say one deliberately built as such, was laid out. A Korean immigrant Roji-no-Takumi erected a model of Mt Sumeru (the mountain lying at the centre of the Buddhist universe supporting the heavens), which consisted of a small mound and a connecting bridge, and included a special building from which it could be viewed. This was followed in 620 by a garden constructed for Soga-no-Umako, which included the first known man-made pond with a small island in it.

These two were important prototypes for later gardens introducing as they did the design elements of a mound, representing a mountain or mountains, and a pond with an island. The islands later came to symbolize a number of ideas depending on their actual shape, but at this stage seem to have represented the Buddhist paradise amongst its seven seas. Alongside these ideas for temple gardens came Chinese temple architecture which included the use of small white stones as a ground covering around the buildings and in the spaces between them.

At the same time as these direct imports were making an appearance, other, less obvious, developments were taking place. These illustrate the way in which existing Japanese concepts and new Buddhist ideas fused to produce something new and individual. Perhaps the clearest example of this was the use of traditional Japanese rock groups to symbolize Buddhist concepts. The specific names and characteristics of various Buddhas were given to suitable rocks or groups of rocks, so that the rocks took on, in some cases, not only their traditional Shinto meaning, but also a Buddhist meaning. For example, large, square stones were named for the

Buddhist deity Fudo (the Immovable), the symbolic protector of Buddhism and its adherents. The 'Fudo' stone was often placed by a waterfall, guarding the source and watching over the water as it passed. Thus, by extension, the water itself, and its course from source to outlet protected by Fudo began to take on various symbolic meanings; the believer passing from his enlightenment, through various trials, to the islands of paradise. Similarly groups of rocks were invested with meaning. A group of three would become the Three Bodies of Buddha (transformation, bliss and law) or an important triad of Buddhas, or more abstract concepts such as heaven, man and earth. In this way the old stone groups became integral parts of the new temple gardens.

Another very important introduction into Japan during this busy period were the Taoist scroll drawings from China. These pen and ink drawings, in the style known as *'sansui'*, reflected the Taoist ideas of man's insignificance amongst the might of nature. *Sansui* means literally 'mountains and water' and the drawings depicted towering mountains with mist-shrouded crags, high waterfalls tumbling into bottomless gorges, roaring torrents, trees clinging to the sides of sheer rock faces and, somewhere below, the tiny figures of men struggling to carry out their work, dwarfed and overpowered by the sheer scale and power of nature. The pictures were a celebration of the wonders of nature and expressed the Taoist belief that man must come to terms with and understand his relative insignificance in the great scheme of nature. It was an idea that the Japanese immediately recognized and understood and the painting techniques and appreciation of the drawings spread rapidly. The drawings were things to be contemplated, the natural world was being promoted as a key to understanding deeper things, and this idea dovetailed with the growing practice of investing rocks and rock groups, gravelled areas and tree groups with specific meaning and importance.

From this time then, gardens were being built that contained the basic elements upon which later developments were based. It is important to note too that right from the beginning, these gardens had a religious meaning, in the sense that they presented the heart of the Buddhist universe and its deities in physical form and were designed to be contemplated. This point is vital to an understanding of later developments and, in particular, to the way in which Zen ideas were incorporated into the designs and how they subtly redirected them.

It was some four hundred years after this initial burst of activity that the next big influence on gardens came into play. During this time, Japan passed from the relative stability of the first emperors into the eras of civil wars. There were continual campaigns for supremacy as the larger military houses vied for power, until Japan settled into the stability of the larger protectorates. Throughout these years there is evidence of a growing dissatisfaction with the highly institutionalized official forms of Buddhism. People without the time or opportunity to undertake the years of study and dedication necessary to gain hopes of salvation through the academic and hierarchical channels of established Buddhist sects, began to search for more direct and accessible ways to relieve the insecurities of life in a country at war within itself, and offer hope for the future. They found it in large numbers in the newly introduced Jodo Pure Land Sect. Introduced around 1175 this sect held that repetition of the Buddha Amida's name would ensure rebirth in his western paradise, the Pure Land (Jodo). It was the kind of populist and simplified movement that periodically appears from within the ranks of most major religions at times of national stress, or when religious leaders have become aloof and inaccessible and the methods of participation too esoteric and difficult.

One of the keys to the success of this particular movement was that the Pure Land in question was not an intellectual concept but was presented as a recognizable physical reality. It was seen as a place where beautiful pavilions stood amongst large ponds full of lotus flowers, and where the immortal souls passed their time in peace and contentment in boats on the ponds, drifting gently amongst the islands and flowers. The emphasis was on immortality in this paradise and longevity in life for those who believed in the redeeming powers of Amida, and this belief was expressed by repetition of his name. Symbolizing this immortality and longevity were the islands in the ponds, based on the old Chinese concept of the isles of the Blest (the blissful dwelling places of immortal ageless beings). Thus the idea of the paradise was central to the whole sect and, to encourage believers by giving them a glimpse of the life to come, it was represented in paintings and drawings full of colour and joy. It was not long before these paintings were turned into reality and gardens specifically based on them were soon being built. In many cases the gardens and ponds were large enough for people actually to use and take boats out amongst the lotus flowers and islands, while musicians played suitable music from the waterside pavilions. Believers were being given a foretaste of what was to come. These

21

gardens although different in scale and uses, were an important stage along the development of later gardens. Present in them were all the elements we have noted already, and they were the grand blueprints from which later developments were taken.

The next stage had to be a reduction in scale and with this a shift back to an emphasis on looking rather than using. These large gardens were doomed from the beginning in the sense that land was becoming scarcer as the towns grew, houses sprang up where once large parks had lain, and by the limitations of what they expressed. As the Pure Land Sect lost ground to newer introductions, particularly the Zen sects, so the grand representations of the Jodo Land became obsolete; other wider, more profound conceptions needed expression. Some of these paradise gardens, notably Kinkakuji in Kyoto, survived and can be seen today more or less exactly as they were built, while others, for example Saiho-ji (Kyoto), underwent transformation at the hands of new priest-gardeners who created new styles within the old, making these gardens particularly interesting to visit.

These new priest-gardeners belonged almost exclusively to one or other of the new Zen Buddhist sects introduced around 1200, and, as we have seen, they had entirely different aims. They had a new approach, developing techniques and ideas that created gardens which are still visited by thousands of visitors every year and which represent for most people the essence of Japanese gardens. For these Zen priests the gardens served a different purpose. They were to be used specifically as aids to deeper understanding of Zen concepts. Gardens were not an end in themselves, as were the Jodo gardens, but were to trigger contemplation and meditation; they were not seen as gardens as such, but rather as spaces filled in a certain way. Abstract compositions relying on understatement, simplicity, suggestion and implication were laid out leaving room for the imagination, but providing a starting point in the appreciation of everyday things. In this there was a return to naturalness and celebration of nature itself. They were trying to present the truths and confusions and problems and joys that man encounters on his path to Zen enlightenment; they were presenting these great concepts not by building on a grand scale as had the followers of Amida, but by reducing the scale, concentrating these ideas into small spaces and gardens around their rooms and temples.

There were two principal ways in which they attempted to do this, and both relied on a reduction of scale for success. One way was to present these things in abstract form, and examples of this range from groups of rock arrangements set apart in moss and trees, as at Saiho-ji, to the ultimate in simplicity as at Ryoanji where fifteen rocks are spread out amongst a flat area of small white stones raked out in lines. The other method originates in the *sansui* drawings from China in which the Taoist ideas of man's place in nature comes very close to Zen ideas of existence. Here the Zen designers were looking for ways to present the vastness of nature and life in a limited space as the *sansui* artists had done. This search led to the building of gardens as at Daisen-in (Kyoto), where a stream falls from the high mountains, passes in swirling currents down through steep gorges and rushes out to flow gently through wider spaces; and this in a small narrow space of some seventy square metres. The method used for this kind of garden was the last great innovation in Japanese gardens and consisted of replacing water with small stones or sand arranged to convey the impression of flowing water. Thus the *sansui* paintings gave rise to the *sansui* styles of garden where mountains and water are used, and the '*karesansui*' (*kare* meaning 'dry') style where substitutes for water were used.

I would like to pause at this point in our brief history of these gardens to emphasize the implications of these developments. By continual blending and absorbing of traditional and new ideas, the Japanese had created by the fourteenth-century gardens of incredible sophistication. They had developed a concept from the first reproductions of Mt Sumeru into a complex art capable of expressing their important religious and philosophical ideas, that created places for rest and recreation, and that would produce an end product that retained power and importance in everyday life some six hundred years later; over and above this, their gardens would capture the imaginations of people all over the world.

The fact that these ideas of garden construction had become an art that could be analysed, written down and handed on, is illustrated by the appearance of books during these years of development that laid down the basic principles for creating gardens. The *Way of Gardening* (the *Sakutei-ki*) and many smaller tracts like it, laid out, complete with drawings, the way in which rocks should be grouped, how 'mountains' should be constructed and what were the general principles of design. Two examples, one straightforward instruction, one containing something more, illustrated this. One passage from the *Way of Gardening* states: 'If you place two rocks in front you always have to follow them up with several others'; and another, illustrating the uniquely Japanese attitude to such simple objects as rocks: 'Rock at the foothills or on plateaux should look like wild dogs staying low, or wild boars running in all directions or small calves playing with their mother.' One gets a feeling from these books of the excitement and creativity that provided the energy behind these years of development, and the latter quotation illustrates how the designers approached their material, seeing in it something more than immediately meets the eye.

Thus, under the influence of Zen, by the late 1200s the basic principles had been established, and from then up to the present day, they have been refined and extended by individual innovators, the most important of whom were connected with *cha-no-yu*, the Japanese tea ceremony. Tea drinking (in this case made from the slightly bitter green tea powder) was introduced into Japan by the Zen priests who drank it to help them stay awake during long hours of meditation. From this beginning it was promoted as a health drink and soon became the centre of social gatherings where it was drunk for recreational purposes. Tea drinking served then, as now, to provide a break from the pressures and hurly-burly of everyday life; and was another offshoot of Zen practices that became central to the Japanese way of life. It provided an opportunity to leave work and the realities of life behind for a while, to sit quietly, reflect, relax and regain some perspective on life. What it meant for the participants is illustrated by an entry in the diary of Kido Takayoshi who was a leading statesman in the later nineteenth century. Writing about a tea ceremony he had attended that day he said: 'I felt as if I had shaken off the cares of this world, and been purified today.' It was a safety valve, a way of relaxing from the rigours of military life in old Japan and serves a similar purpose now in present-day Japan for those caught up in the intensity of modern urban and industrial living. Tea and the ritualized form of making and drinking it became an integral part of Japanese life and the tea-masters (the men who served tea for the emperors, and who refined and passed on the details of the ceremony) exerted an enormous influence on the development of Japanese culture as a whole and specifically, for our purposes, on the design of gardens. They were also for the most part Zen priests of one sect or another.

Almost as important as the tea itself was the teahouse in which it was served and the garden in which the house stood. The teahouse, its design and contents, was vital to create the correct atmosphere. They were usually small, very simple wooden structures, valued for their simplicity and the way in which they embodied the spirit of nature and naturalness. Made of basic materials, undecorated and essentially bare, the houses, which in many cases were little more than huts, were complemented by the unsophisticated and almost plain fittings, tea bowls and utensils; they cut away the pretensions, vulgarity and unnaturalness of the commercial world.

The tea gardens surrounding or leading up to the houses were designed for the same purpose. Known as the *roji* ('dewy path') these served to help people shake off the everyday life they had just left, to settle their minds and prepare them for entering the teahouse. Often there was a small open-fronted waiting room where guests could sit, relax and enter into the spirit and atmosphere of the place. Once inside, weather permitting, an open screen might provide glimpses of the pool, or shrubs, the colours in the sunlight, the wind in the leaves, or let in the sounds of a small waterfall or carp jumping in deeper pools. These *roji* were some of the first really small-scale gardens and in them were used for the first time some of the objects that have become synonymous with Japanese gardens. The water bowls, used initially for rinsing hands and mouth before entering the teahouse, and the stone lanterns, to light the way in the evening, have now become an integral part of gardens and have taken on an ornamental function.

More important, however, than this introduction of ornaments was the way in which the designers of the tea gardens extended the range and concept of garden designs. Following directly from the arrangements of utensils and the layout of the teahouse for the ceremonies, came the ideas of design based on diagonals, assymmetry and the reusing of objects in different ways. The use of diagonals and assymmetric design came from the irregular arrangement of utensils which would be placed round the tea-maker and fireplace in triangular groups rather than square or rectangular ones (Figure 1).

In the field of design, symmetry was seen as a deadend; it held no surprises, no mystery. Thus a diagonal approach to the house was introduced, the paths were laid without form so that during a stroll along them you never know what you will see or where you will end up. In smaller gardens these principles were used for the arrangement of rocks and governed the relationships between groups and their relationship to the path or building. On a larger scale they guided the construction of waterfalls and fell in with the Japanese aesthetic principle of breaking symmetry to harmonize with nature. Ornaments made from cut stone, such as water bowls, would be deliberately chipped to offset the effect of the severe lines of the cuts

25

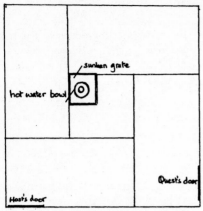

1a.   This shows the arrangement of mats in a four-and-a-half-mat tearoom. One section of the centre mat has been removed and the bowl for hot water placed on the sunken charcoal fire. The host's door leads in from the small room where the utensils are kept, and the guest's door from the garden.

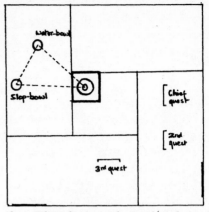

1b.   When the guests have taken their places, the host will enter with the first utensils, the water bowl and slop bowl, and positon them as shown. The triangle thus formed provides the framework within which the other utensils are placed.

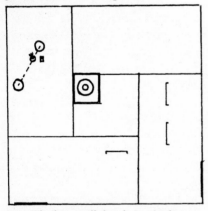
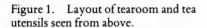

1c.   The host will then bring in the tea bowl, with the whisk placed in it, and the tea caddy. These are stood near the water bowl, starting with the tea bowl on the left-hand side of the triangle.

Figure 1.   Layout of tearoom and tea utensils seen from above.

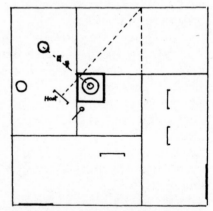

1d.   Once the host has knelt in position and started making tea, the whisk and the caddy are repositioned down the right-hand side of the triangle, and the water ladle is laid down parallel to the direction in which the host is facing. There are a number of moves for the utensils as the ceremony progresses, but it can be seen from these preliminary positions how the layout and approach is governed by triangular and diagonal shapes.

26

and permit one to see the natural textures of the stone. The idea of reusing things promoted the discovery of new uses and beauty in objects that had been discarded or no longer served their original purpose. This particularly applies to building materials, stones or wood reused for paths or fences.

As has already been noted, the influence of these designers on Japanese life has been so profound that we cannot pass on without mentioning a few by name. For visitors to present day Kyoto (the former capital of Japan, that was unaffected by the destruction of the Second World War and where the greatest concentration of old gardens can still be seen) who read their guide books as they visit the various gardens, the names of two designers will appear again and again: Soseki (Musokokushi) and Kobori Enshu.

Soseki (1275–1351) was undoubtedly the most important figure in medieval garden design. His work marks the real watershed between the traditional and Pure-Land forms of gardens and the later gardens that developed under the influence of Zen and the tea ceremony. He was a Zen priest and one of the designers who wanted to interpret the *sansui* painting style. His gardens include the large pond and waterfall arrangement at Tenryuji (Kyoto), the compact small garden at Toji-in (Kyoto), where steep banks of shrubs fall to a small pond with an island and a bridge and, perhaps his greatest of all, the moss gardens at Saiho-ji (Kyoto). It was Soseki who transformed this garden from the lotus pond/pavilion style of the Pure Land Sect to the rock groups and stroll paths amidst the simplicity and quietness of the Zen style. He removed the pavilions, altered the buildings, broke up the large pond with a network of islands. He divided the garden into two, creating a *karesansui* rock garden in the upper half and a more classic garden based around the pond in the lower. The entire garden at Saiho-ji is carpeted with more than a hundred kinds of moss. An important point to notice here was the dividing of the garden. Whereas in previous times the large gardens had been intended for large groups of people to gather, for entertainment and relaxation, the Zen gardens were private. They were a place for the priests to go, alone, uninterrupted, to meditate, to gain enlightenment. The gardens came to be screened off from the world by walls, intricate fences or stands of bamboo. This idea developed too in the teahouse *roji* and they were the forerunners of present-day urban gardens: small private plots where the owners can escape the world for a while in privacy.

It is not possible to know what Soseki had in mind as he created the rock arrangement at Saiho-ji. What he saw was a medium by which he could help students to understand the Zen truth. The point to note here is that he was using rocks and garden space in a new way, a way specific enough to aid in his role as teacher, and yet abstract enough to become part of the larger world of gardens and bring enjoyment to thousands of different people. It is a design that transcends his period and country. Like all the reductions of scale that occurred around this time, he was using the small space and the rocks in it as a form of shorthand to express the essence of the natural world, the twists and turns of people's lives, the equally contorted 'way' to enlightenment, and the difficulties faced by every student of Zen. Rather than having specific meaning they were a catalyst to thought, an invitation to and guide during meditation. The gardens became places for personal discoveries not, as were the Pure-Land gardens, public parks for the celebration of a truth everyone believed in. In this way, the concepts of suggestion and implication, of one thought leading to another, were introduced into the designs of Japanese gardens.

Kobori Enshu was building gardens during the early seventeenth century, and they are dotted all over the ancient capital Kyoto. A prolific all-round designer and influential tea-master, he favoured bright and open gardens, places that were a pleasure to be in. He had a considerable influence on the designs of gateways, ornaments such as lanterns, and the shapes and patterns of windows in walls or teahouses. His gardens follow the general concepts that we have discussed but it is for his innovations and refinements of the '*shakkei*' technique that he is chiefly remembered. *Shakkei* (literally 'borrowed' scenery) combined with either *sansui* or *karesansui* styles is another vital element in basic Japanese garden design. Dating back to the gardens of the early emperors and feudal lords, this technique involves the deliberate inclusion of some natural feature outside the garden in the overall design. Maybe a distant line of hills, or a prominent mountain or a view across a valley would be easily visible from a garden, and, by leaving gaps in the planting or constructing low walls and fences, this feature could be included in the garden itself. It is a very useful technique since it enables one to add depth and a sense of space to small gardens and helps blend the garden into its surroundings.

Finally, no look at the development of Japanese gardens would be complete without a mention of Sen-no-Rikkyu (1520–91), perhaps the greatest of all the tea-masters and one of the outstanding arbitrators of aesthetic tastes in the history of Japanese culture.

Inheriting ideas directly from the earliest tea-masters of the previous century, he almost single-handedly defined the rituals and associated arts of tea drinking with such skill and authority that they remain almost unchanged to the present day.

This is not to imply that the tea ceremony in Japan today is a moribund copying of Rikkyu for his own sake, but rather that he established standards and attitudes that remained relevant, inspiring and flexible enough to retain their importance amidst the changes in Japanese life, and that can still answer people's needs today. This applies also to his innovations in the field of gardening. He was not a builder on a large scale as Soseki had been or Enshu was to be, instead he left his indelible mark on the design of the teahouse *rojis*. He preferred the dewy paths to be narrow, closed in, more compact and immediate in their impact. He filled small areas, designing within the existing limitations of space, an approach which proved crucial for garden development. After Rikkyu, anyone, from the greatest to the humblest, in big or small, convenient or awkward spaces could create a garden. His ideas, representing the refinement of all that had gone before can be seen today in the streets of Japan's cities and indeed in many countries throughout the world. He was also responsible for integrating such ornaments as lanterns into regular garden designs.

So by the late seventeenth century the process of development was complete. From the initial impetus created by the introduction of Buddhism, through the changes brought about by the different styles of religion, and passing finally into the hands of individuals inspired by Zen and under the continual influence of native ideas, a style of gardening had been created that was uniquely Japanese. For the next few hundred years under the rule of the great military regents (known as *shoguns*) Japan remained sealed off from any outside influences. No new religious or artistic ideas entered the country. It was not until the restoration of the Meiji Emperor in the 1880s and the subsequent opening up of Japan by Western traders, that new ideas began again to be seen in nearly every aspect of administrative and governmental business; but the art and culture of Japan remained almost unaffected. Particularly, the wide, rolling parklands planted with mighty trees, or the geometric flower gardens and ornamental ponds and fountains, or indeed the lawns and flower beds, of Western gardens, were to have little impact on a crowded Zen-influenced Japan.

It may appear from this history that gardening in Japan was limited to people of great wealth, emperors and their courtiers and the large temples; people and institutions with plenty of land and money to pay for the creation of pools, mountains, pavilions and boating parties. Initially this was true, but with the breakup of imperial power, and the subsequent broadening of political power bases amongst the large military houses there occurred a wide extension of participation in all aspects of life. This extension, with the consolidation of land ownership, a certain amount of leisure, and the close participation of the populace in the developing religions, coupled with the work of people like Soseki, Rikkyu and large numbers of other designers who reduced the scale of gardens, made it possible for people right across the social scale to build and enjoy their own gardens. Small plots that represent the refinement of several hundred years of development. It is on this kind of scale that this book hopes to pass on some of the ideas and techniques that make up this garden art, to help people make the most of awkward corners of large gardens, plots not large enough for lawns and beds, or passageways, alleys and terraces.

We have looked at our two secondary themes, the development of Zen Buddhism and the development of the gardens, and how the two came together to create our main theme, 'Zen gardening'. I want now to take a detailed look at the various elements that actually make up the gardens, focusing in turn on the different components.

It is worth noting at this point, however, that generally speaking, the overall design of gardens is achieved by linking various groups of components together – gardens in Japan are looked at, or appreciated, in rather the same way as the long, rolled-up scroll paintings that so influenced their development. A garden is rarely designed to be seen all at once from a single viewpoint. Rather, small, differing scenes open up as one passes along the paths. Similarly, the scrolls were not seen all at once like conventional pictures, but unrolled with one hand and rolled up with the other as each changing scene is appreciated. The shorter, hanging scrolls, also tend to lead the eye up or down through different scenes that do not necessarily have a total overall continuity. With this in mind, we can pass on to a close look at what makes up these groups in gardens and what is used to join them.

2

The Garden Components and Their Adaptation

We shall look first at the components for a basic *sansui* (mountain and water) garden, and then at variations for *karesansui* (dry mountain and water) style, and finally at variations for either style if the garden includes a *shakkei* ('borrowed scenery') view. This section is a review of types and background details, rather than design details, which will be covered fully in Chapter 3, 'Principles of Design'.

The word 'mountain' here may be rather confusing. What we are talking about in fact is earth mounds built up to represent the mountains, or high land, from which the streams fall towards the lower ground, the plains and eventually the sea. In effect, on our reduced scale, these mounds form the background for the garden, against which is set the pool or lower planting. They provide also the height for a waterfall, and are supported behind by dense back planting, to create a sense of remoteness and depth (Figure 2). It is clearly impossible in an average or small-sized garden to re-create complete scale mountains or mountain ranges, and so the intention is to re-create some aspect of a mountain: a ridge or crag, either real or most probably imaginary. If the mounds are to create a waterfall then, of course, attention is focused on this feature and the mounds built away on either side to give sufficient bulk and visual support to the construction. If a path is to lead round or up a mound then again attention must be paid to visible faces. If the mound is to be visible from all sides then it will be designed along the lines of a free-standing rockery, a natural-looking combination of stones and earth.

In gardens where water is already present, or can relatively easily be introduced, it may be included in the designs in a variety of ways. It can be used in the classic style being fed down a waterfall, along a stream course and into a pool (often being pumped from there back up to the waterfall). Alternatively, existing streams can be used to fill

31

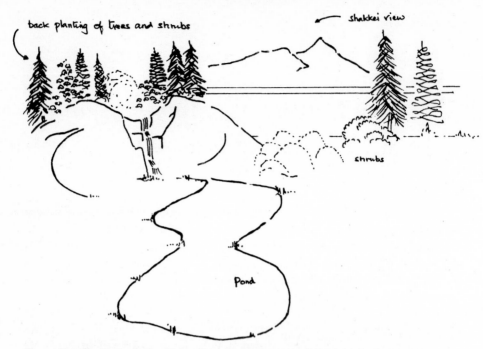

Figure 2. Illustrates the basic concept of built-up mounds with back planting, the waterfall leading into the pond and the spaces left in boundary planting to allow for the view behind.

pools or fed through the garden from one side and to the other. Gardens without water, or where it is impossible to introduce due to size or other reasons, should be designed in *karesansui* style which is discussed later. It should be noted, however, that in present-day gardens, developed as we have seen from the smaller temple and tea gardens after the 1200s, that the presence of water, either real or symbolic, is the important thing, not necessarily the quantity, and that water features can in fact be very small, shallow and compact and still be effective. Water should not be counted out straightaway.

If a waterfall is to be included it must be designed and built with the utmost care. A well-designed waterfall forming the focal point for a garden can give hours of pleasure in all seasons as the water bounces and splashes in spring, trickles and sparkles in summer, and drips to form icicles in winter. The sounds and movement of a waterfall can bring a garden alive, whatever its size, and this goes a long way to explain their importance for the Japanese designers. The crucial factor, of course, in a successful waterfall is the placing of the stones down which the water will fall. It is interesting to note that the full Japanese name for a waterfall is *taki-ishi-gimi* which literally means 'stone' (*ishi*) 'pathway' (*gimi*) 'for falling water' (*taki*) and that the alternate reading for the characters is *ryiou* which means 'a dragon'. Thus the stone pathway is as important as the water, and the combined effect of both is compared to the twirling, flashing coils of a dragon's body. Correctly built waterfalls can give this impression, while a badly designed fall can seem lifeless and uninteresting, in spite of the movement of water. Waterfalls, like ponds, require considerable time to be spent on imaginative planning but can be very rewarding once built.

As has already been pointed out, water features, streams or ponds do not have to be large or deep to have effect. A small, suitably planted pond can be every bit as interesting as a larger one. In Japan the pond is often considered as the 'heart' of the garden, the *kokoro* (literally 'the heart of things'), and to convey this impression they are often designed to be either roughly heart-shaped or to represent the ideogram for 'shin' or 'new heart'. As with so many garden components, the Japanese give the pond a particular poetic feeling, such as the waterfall 'dragons'. In this case it is useful from a design point of view to think of the pond as the heart of the garden. In other words, design should first concentrate on the pond and its immediate setting and then work outwards to blend in the rest of the garden. The construction of ponds need not be complicated, since even the larger ones in Japan are rarely very deep, but before finalizing designs careful thought should be given to how the pond will be used – is it just for planting, or will it contain fish, an island or even a bridge? Will a waterfall feed directly into it, if not, where is the source of water, where is the outlet and so on? We will be looking at these points in more detail in Chapter 4, but I will take a quick look now at some of the features associated with ponds.

Islands, as we have already seen, have a particular importance for the Japanese. They are representative of the isles of the Blest where the immortal souls live. For the living, they represent a symbol of longevity and continuing health and are thus often used as the focal points for ponds, or as a counterpoint to a waterfall in the overall balancing of a pond design. In the West islands have a similar mythological tradition in the old Celtic culture, but nowadays their role would be to add interest to a pond design. For small ponds an island need only be a single rock carefully positioned to give an interesting shape above water level. The rock can represent a steep

Figure 3a.   Single-rock island.   Figure 3b.   Island built up of rocks and
                                           earth and then planted.

craggy stack (following the kind of rocks shown in *sansui* paintings)
or can be a larger, flatter rock representing an altogether larger
island. In larger ponds it can be built up of a number of rocks, filled
with earth and planted, creating a feature that will add depth and
detail to the pond (Figure 3). A third type can be made large enough
to support one end of a bridge which again adds interest to the pond.
A large number of ponds in Japan feature both single rocks and
built-up islands and the latter often take the shape of two prominent
symbols of longevity: the tortoise (which is believed to live for
10,000 years) and the crane (which lives for a thousand). Whether or
not these ages have ever been proved, these shapes are very popular
and their design is outlined in Chapter 3.

Bridges have a number of clear functions, like taking a path across
a pond, opening up alternative viewpoints that might otherwise not
exist, leading out to an island, or connecting one island to another.
But above all, providing their scale suits the pond size, they can open
up the pond itself and give visual cohesion to the overall design. In
Japan, garden bridges were traditionally constructed of a single uncut
piece of stone, slightly arched if possible to give a more pleasing
effect.

To find such stones was both expensive and difficult, and gradu-
ally during the later, more creatively freer periods of design after the
fifteenth century, other forms of bridges became equally acceptable.
After 1600 bridges of cut stone began to be used and in the shorthand
typical of Japanese gardeners other materials came to represent
different kinds of bridges. For example a passage in the *Way of
Gardening* states that bridges made of natural stone (Figure 4a) are
used to suggest a scene of a swift stream tumbling down a mountain
ravine. On the other hand bridges made of wood and earth (Figure
4b) suggest a stream passing through a village, while bridges of
wood or cut stone (Figure 4c) represent an urban scene, or a river

passing through a town. Inevitably, cut stones tend to look rather straight and square and can dominate a small informal pool, but used on the right scale they can also be very pleasing.

The choice of bridge material will depend on personal taste, availability of materials and desired effect, but some general design points that apply to any kind of bridge, must be borne in mind. Bridges should not only be strong and secure, they should also *look* strong and secure. Thus the span across the water is supported and backed up by stones that anchor and hold it. These 'bridge-supporting' stones play a very important role in the overall design of a bridge. They add balance and solidity to counteract the sweep and grace of the span stretching out over the water. The quantity, size and positioning of these stones is detailed in Chapter 3.

Rocks have two main functions. On the one hand they have an intrinsic beauty of their own, and on the other they can represent something altogether larger and more universal. In the first place they bring something of the countryside and the mountains into

Figure 4.   Different types of bridges.

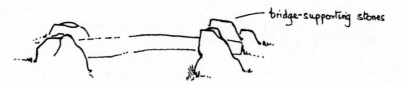

a. Single span of uncut, lightly arching stone.

b. Combination of wood and earth – a village scene.

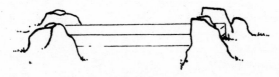

c. Single span of cut stone – a town scene.

town gardens and their colours and shapes are a pleasure to look at. A well-weathered rock with its covering of moss is something which can never be reproduced using other materials; it is unique and solid, an unchanging focus amongst the passing of the year around it. Alternatively, looking past the immediate rock, it can be seen as representing the more massive aspects of nature which cannot be realistically translated or otherwise introduced into a garden, particularly a small one. The rocks form the basic key to the gardener's shorthand. The swirling, twisted strata or a single rock, or the flowing, asymmetrical relationship of a group of rocks can transmit to those observing in a meditative mood the more spiritual aspects of life, the ups and downs and the difficulties of human relationships, the rough and the smooth. Rocks as much as the earth around them are the foundation of the garden. For rocks to fulfil these roles, however, two points of design should be established. We have already seen that traditionally rocks have been grouped in certain numbers. The basic triad stems from the religious importance of the number three (similar to the all-important three of the Christian trinity) and other groups, for example five and seven, are based round other important numbers. (The beautiful garden at Shoden-ji temple (Kyoto), has clipped azaleas arranged in a seven-five-three pattern, which is a common variation of the 'rock-group' theme.) Apart from the traditional importance of these numbers they also ensure that groups are arranged in uneven numbers. This means that the groupings will never be noticeably symmetrical and thus fulfills the basic requirement of Japanese garden design that overall and component design should be asymmetrical, breaking up straight lines, squares and regular shapes.

The second point, perhaps one of the most interesting aspects of Japanese rock work, is the way in which standard rock shapes were identified (and later codified in the old garden books) making it possible to introduce all the basic shapes of natural rock formations. In the same way as they studied how water fell and defined various basic designs for waterfalls, the old gardeners of Japan identified four basic rock shapes: tall and thin, large and squat, arching and flat (see Figures 5a, b, c, d). (It is from these shapes that the more poetic descriptions of rocks, such as reclining or running dogs, calves following their mother and even a tiger and her cubs, have arisen.) These five basic shapes, with the occasional addition of any particularly attractive or interestingly shaped stone, are the basis of all the groupings found in Japanese gardens, and in Chapter 3, 'Principles of

a. Tall, thin rock type.

b. Large, squat rock type.

c. Arching rock type.

d. Flat rock type.

Figure 5.   Four basic rock shapes.

Design', we shall see how these shapes are used to form the rock groups.

Although this method of using rocks may seem somewhat involved and confusing there are some guiding rules on which it is based, and a knowledge of these makes the job really very simple. One, as we have seen, is that there are basic rock shapes, and the other is that groups should be formed in a particular way, starting with one stone and working out around or in front of it. This will be covered fully in Chapter 3, but the quick analysis of the basic group, the triad, will indicate how it works. In the triad there are three stones: the central stone (*shuseki*), the first subordinate (*fukuseki*) and the second subordinate (*kyakuseki*). Since the *shuseki* is the most important and generally the largest, this is placed first. The *fukuseki* follows, its different shape and size balancing and complementing the *shuseki*, and finally the *kyakuseki* is used to fill out and complete the design. Other groups, five or seven, usually start with the basic three and are then built out with 'supporting' stones to form the larger groups. This systematic and organized method of building

37

helps to make the rock work both fascinating and relatively simple. Not as difficult as it may sound.

As I have previously pointed out, most Japanese gardens are to be looked at, and to get the most out of them they usually have more than one viewing point. Thus an important component in garden design are the paths that link the different views. In the west a garden path tends to be functional and necessary in the sense that it conveys someone or something through the garden, providing a clean, flat, dry place to walk. They are usually a means of getting from one place to another (house to gate, or garage to shed and so on). In the garden itself the lawn usually provides access to flower beds or fruit trees. In Japan paths often begin and end in the same place: they, instead of lawns, are the vital linking factor, joining garden groups, providing access, and offering a variety of views as one progresses around the garden.

They are made of a wide variety of materials and, rather like bridges, can be used to express certain moods, or suggest certain settings: a beaten-earth path through the shrubs and trees might suggest a walk in the mountains or countryside, while an elaborately designed, regular stone path suggests something more organized and urban. Again, paths can be either continual or broken like stepping stones. Stepping-stone paths were most commonly used in tea gardens where their irregularity, broken shapes and overall informality helped to create an atmosphere that contrasted with the more regular streets outside the gate. Paths can be of infinite variety, formal or informal, drawing attention to themselves by particularly striking designs, and standing out in contrast to the surrounding plants, or blending in to be almost unnoticeable as you walk along. Another important factor of the paths' surface is the sound it makes as you walk over it. Going right back to the early shrines we looked at in the history of the gardens, sound has been an integral part of design. In the same way as wind in the trees, birds calling, the splash and gurgle of the waterfall or stream, the crunch of a gravel path helps to set the garden apart.

There is a similar tradition in Western gardening of using paths for different purposes, although like so many aspects of western garden design, it belongs more to the era of large country-house landscaping which, unlike in Japan, was never reduced to a smaller scale in a way that would continue to play an important role in modern design. One aspect though, the differentiation between paths or drives leading up to the house, and the smaller garden paths has survived. The drive was created to be self-consciously grand, building up the expectations of the visitor as the house was approached. It served to separate the house and its immediate surroundings from the outside world. The wide sweeps and bends of the grand tradition can still be recognized in the drives of many houses today. These drives were laid with a specific purpose in mind in much the same way and with the same attention to detail as the smallest garden path in a Japanese garden.

Turning now from the basic makeup of the gardens, we shall look at two final important groups of components that are used to focus the design and bring them to life: the ornaments and the plants.

The objects in Japanese gardens that could be described as ornaments all began life with a practical purpose. Some still retain much of this original purpose, while others have become in the full sense of the word 'ornamental'. Even though for many people it is the ornaments themselves that suggest that a garden is Japanese, being the most readily recognizable aspects of the gardens, they are very few in number and are included in the design for very specific purposes.

The most important of these ornaments are the lanterns and water bowls, while other objects, less frequently introduced, include *stupas* ('stone towers'), *sozu* ('bamboo tippers') and very occasionally stone or metal figures. Basically the Japanese believe that you cannot improve on nature and therefore that you should not try to decorate it in unnatural ways; thus, as we've seen, their ornaments were basically or theoretically functional and even if some have now become ornamental they are still symbolic of their original purpose and most indeed could still be used for it if required.

The Japanese stone lantern developed from the brass lantern designs of ancient China. It consists of a covered lamp stand supported on a column, often all cut from one stone. The candle, or taper is placed in the stand and paper placed in the sides to make it windproof, and the whole unit was often ornately decorated.

Traditionally these lanterns were found in temples and shrines, where they served a number of purposes. Many were used for their light at gateways, in doorways, or lining the approaches to the buildings. Some more ornate ones were ornaments for particular ceremonies, only being lit when required, and some were used as memorials, the candle burning in memory of the dead. More generally lanterns were used at crossroads or in larger houses, but their origins were in the religious centres.

In the early days of gardens, lanterns were sometimes introduced for their light and often because people wanted to create something of the atmosphere of a shrine or temple around their house. The big moss-covered lanterns introduced some of the quiet, tranquil timelessness that was such an important part of people's lives. They conveyed something of the feeling of solidity and continuity that is so much a part of the atmosphere in the old cathedrals and monasteries of Europe, in a country where the buildings were wooden and therefore more temporary and subject to fire or change.

But the history of stone lanterns in gardens really begins with the work of the tea master Sen-no-Rikkyu who caused them to become a major element in garden makeup right to this day. Rikkyu began to use them in his teahouse gardens because he liked the light they gave. He considered their dim, gentle but rich light ideal to create the right atmosphere for an evening tea ceremony. After this, lanterns slowly became permanent features in the gardens that developed out of the *roji* style because, typical of the man, he not only introduced the idea, but he also simplified the designs, often building them up of uncut, undecorated stones and so opened the way for anyone to create their own.

Before Rikkyu lanterns tended to be large, ornate affairs and the different designs were named after the shrine or temple where they originated. Thus we have for example the 'Kasuga' style and the 'Nigatsudokata' style, named after the two shrines in Nara where they were developed (Figure 6a and b). These are found in shrines and temples as well as in gardens.

After Rikkyu a wide range of styles, on the whole less elaborate and ornate, were developed by and named after leading tea-masters (see Figure 7a, b, c). In this way, we have, to name a few, Rikkyu, Oribe and Enshu lanterns (Oribe like Rikkyu and Enshu was an important and influential tea-master and garden designer). These types of lanterns are used in many gardens but not in the shrines or temples.

In addition to the above, there are a number of lantern designs named after their shape, and which cannot be ascribed to individual people or places. The most popular of these, and perhaps the best-known, most typically Japanese lantern today, is the *yuki-mi-doro* ('snow-viewing lantern') (Figure 7d), so called because its wide, flattish top allows snow to settle in depth. Another example of this type is the *hakaku-doro* ('eight-sided lantern') (Figure 7e) which tends to be located at the junctions of paths, since it throws light in a number of directions.

Today these lanterns retain their importance, whether for their

a. Kasuga-style lantern.   b. Nigatsudokata-style lantern.

Figure 6.   Both these lanterns are named after the temples they originated from and illustrated the elaborate, highly ornate styles of ceremonial lanterns. They should be compared with the simpler and more basic styles of the tea-masters' lanterns shown in Figure 7.

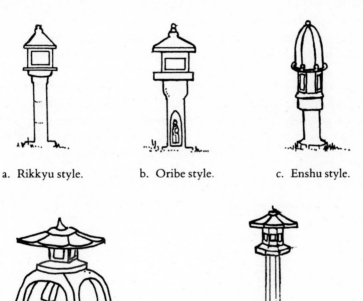

a. Rikkyu style.   b. Oribe style.   c. Enshu style.

d. *Yuki-mi-doro:* snow viewing lantern.   e. *Hakaku-doro:* the eight-sided lantern style.

Figure 7.   Although the tea-masters designed many different lanterns, some of natural and some of cut stones, these examples illustrate the general proportions and shapes preferred by each.

41

light or as ornaments, and are a central feature of many gardens, either standing alone or grouped with a bowl.

Similarly water bowls have developed from practical origins to become important ornaments, although rather more than lanterns they have retained their original pupose. *Chōzubachi* (literally 'reservoir basins'), were originally placed in front of shrines and later temples, for worshippers to wash their hands and rinse their mouths before entering. The bowls were usually made of cut stone (see Figure 8a) and stood some two or three feet high, similar to modern wash basins, for convenient washing. Their origins date back to the earliest times when the presence of water was vital for purification at the old shrines. Today, they continue to serve the same purpose and because of their symbolic importance have become a feature of gardens as well.

When the tea-masters of the middle ages designed their tea houses and gardens they included water bowls so that guests could wash their hands before entering for the ceremony. They redesigned the bowls, however, and created the *tsukubai* ('crouching bowl') to suit the different atmosphere and purpose of the tea garden (Figure 8b). Instead of being made of large cut stones, the *tsukubai* were very low and made use of natural indentations in the stone. The idea was that the guest had to crouch down to wash, to humble himself and so help create the right state of mind before joining the ceremony. Rikkyu considered the act of crouching extremely important since it presents things in a different way; people often appreciate things more if they are not immediately apparent or accessible.

Figure 8.

a. The *chōzubachi*, the cut stone style of water bowl.

b. The *tsukubai*, waterbowl using the natural hollow of an uncut stone.

Many gardens today contain both *chōzubachi* and *tsukubai* and occasionally the bowls are fed with fresh water from a bamboo spout, overflowing into a soakaway at their base. The arrangement of the groups will be analysed in Chapter 3.

There are two other types of ornament that should be mentioned; the *stupa* and the *sōzu*. *Stupa*s are stone towers, looking something like a multistoried pagoda, that represent the one standing at the place where Buddha was buried. They are thus both a memorial to the Buddha and, by extension, symbols of the Buddhist faith. Many now serve also as memorials to individual people and can be seen in any size from about ten feet to smaller ones of two or three feet (Figure 9a).

As ornaments in the garden they serve as focal points for views or to help give a sense of distance. A small *stupa* for example, placed in a suitably scaled setting can look much further away than it actually is. They can be found in a wide variety of designs and, like the stone lanterns, are a well-known feature of Japanese gardens. Although to many westerners these ornaments are synonymous with the gardens, it should be rememberd that for the Japanese and their garden designs, the ornaments are not of primary importance. They are usually included for a specific purpose and are rarely purely decorative; the gardens themselves, the design and planting are the most important thing.

Figure 9a.   *Stupa*: a stone memorial tower.

Figure 9b.   *Sozu*: a bamboo tipper fed with water from a small spout. When full the tube tips forward, empties, and swings back to its original position, hitting the stone with a 'clack'. The process then repeats itself.

The *sōzu* (Figure 9b) are an interesting survival of old agricultural techniques, and were introduced into gardens for both practical and aesthetic reasons. They consist of a bamboo tube fitted to tip on legs, which is continually filled with water. When the tube fills up it tips forward, empties and falls back into its original position. As it lands back it strikes a stone making a loud 'clack'. It was thus used by farmers as an animal and bird scarer, and served the same purpose in gardens. It was even capable of scaring away the wild boars that inhabited the closely forested mountains, and which occasionally foraged on farm land. It is an unusual and easily made ornament and its regular, rather mournful, clacking was considered to be a suitable accompaniment while contemplating the garden.

While the *sōzu* and other ornaments add atmosphere to the garden, the next group of components we shall look at – walls, fences and screens – help to provide the framework and setting for it. For the Japanese there is a big difference between the function of a wall and a fence. The solid bulk of an earth or stone wall is not generally used within the garden but rather around the boundary, to cut out the outside world and make the garden as private and peaceful as possible. On the other hand, partition within the garden is achieved with various kinds of fences and screens using light, frailer-looking materials such as bamboo or brushwood (see Figures 68–73). Anything as permanent and durable as stone walls in the garden would be seen as cutting across the delicately natural atmosphere where the emphasis is on impermanence: the passing seasons, the blooming and fading of flowers, spring and autumn leaves, the continual movement of water. In addition, screens in particular, are designed to suggest shapes and spaces in the garden, rather than creating actual barriers. Generally, one can get glimpses of what is behind or beyond them. Another function of the screens is to provide a backdrop for a particular arrangement, a water-bowl group for example, highlighting it and giving the group a degree of seclusion and self-containment.

Choice of materials for a wall, fence or screen depends largely on its function and exactly how much of a division is required to separate the various parts of the garden, and we shall be looking at a number of different types and the jobs they can do in Chapter 3.

Finally in this section on garden components, we'll take a quick look at plants. This book does not cover the actual planting, trimming or care of plants or trees, but covers types and guidelines on what to plant and where to plant it. Generally speaking the planting of the garden should aim to be as natural as possible. It should try to create the impression of a natural setting by providing detail and some depth. Overplanting, or trees and shrubs planted too thickly should be avoided, since this introduces a feeling of stiff unnaturalness and will tend to overpower the other features of the garden. A pool and stream, or a mountain stream and waterfall, should be planted with things that suggest the setting and any regularity or symmetry of planting should be carefully avoided. Another point worth noting is that if the garden has fine views or is surrounded by particular trees or shrubs of interest, then these should be blended in as much as possible. This avoids any feeling of artificiality, which is the key to successful design.

Similarly anything that would create a discordant note by being too large or too bright and colourful should be left out because, apart from being unnatural, it would also detract from the other features. In some cases a particularly fine miniature or beautiful cherry tree may be a special feature but only if they fit the general scale of the garden. This is not to say that planting should aim to be bland and colourless, but that care should be taken to maintain scale and the overall impression.

Plants and trees in Japanese gardens have a number of specific purposes, but they, like other features and ornaments, are rarely purely decorative. Perhaps the most important role they play is of giving a background and general cohesion to the design. They support and join the various components creating the overall impression and mood. On the other hand, in gardens designed to have a number of different viewing points, the plants can act as dividers that separate the various scenes and at the same time provide backgrounds. This kind of planting will need to be denser and more solid to be convincing. A third use of plants is for screening and this is an idea at the very heart of the landscaping art. Particularly in small gardens it is the power of suggestion that makes them work; the suggestion that the garden is in fact part of something much bigger, like a ravine on a mountainside, or a waterfall forming part of a stream's course. In addition to this, careful screen planting can make the garden seem bigger, as though it contains more than it actually does. This is particularly true when branches are trained out over the pool, allowing only glimpses of what is behind. Detail is implied rather than actually present and the observer is free to imagine more. Screening is a case where the plants or trees are an integral part of the design, they are not featured so much as used for framing or adding to the other elements. This technique, and indeed the other points we have looked at here, are equally valid for gardens with or without water.

This section has been intended to introduce some general thoughts about the use of plants and their place in the gardens.

A list of suitable plants and their uses will be found in Appendix 2, p. 148, and planting ideas accompany the different layouts suggested in the second half of Chapter 3. For detailed guidance on planting and cultivation more specialized books on this subject should be consulted.

We have now looked in some detail at the basic components for a *sansui*-style garden; one that has water in it in some form. For the *karesansui*-style (dry mountain and water gardens) the components are basically the same as for above except there is no actual water flowing or filling the pond.

Dry landscapes are built in places that are too small to include water, where it is too technically difficult to introduce it or where it is a matter of preference (since dry gardens require less maintainence than those with water), but where people would like to introduce the idea of water. It is a way to bring the suggestion of water to waterless places. In this way water substitutes are used to represent a pool or stream flowing between the rocks and trees. An additional point is that some substitutes, such as gravel or small stones, look like the dried-up bed of a stream or pool, suggesting that after rain the water will flow again. In the same way, the stones used for the waterfall not only substitute for water but give the impression that water might flow down them again at any moment. Thus the dry landscapes substitute for the absence of water, and suggest that this is only temporary.

46

An additional, more general point should also be made here, which is that to a large extent, the juxtapositioning of detail and blank spaces is a very old concept that goes back to the *sansui* paintings of China and runs up through the later Zen ideas of art. On the scroll paintings as much of the paper was left blank (white) as was actually drawn on. This took the scene out of any particular context, left room for the imagination to fit the time, place and surroundings. Similarly the temple gardens of the Zen sects are invariably in *karesansui* style with large areas of white gravel substituting for water, and also setting off similar contrasts between the details of the trees and rocks and the white spaces that surround them. This is more a theoretical point than an actual design guideline but it is one of the important background ideas that help one to design along Japanese lines.

Clearly, the most important component of the *karesansui* style is the water substitute. The most readily available and convenient one is gravel since it is easy to obtain and lay, but small white stones or chippings are suitable if they can be obtained. Other good substitutes include moss and grass either seed or turf. Whatever material is used, it is laid on level ground in shapes that suggest streams or ponds and then edged with rocks and plants. If gravel or stones are used then the surface can be raked to suggest the ripples and eddies of moving water. Features like islands and bridges are planned and built exactly as they would be for water, and then the 'water' is laid around or under them. It is surprising just how impressive, and in its way, realistic, this *karesansui* style can look. Needless to say, channelling, retaining and controlling water is more expensive than laying a substitute.

Other garden components should be approached and designed exactly as though there was water present. Using a substitute does not alter the way in which the garden is planned and constructed, although it may make it simpler. On the other hand if the garden, whether wet or dry, is to include the *shakkei* technique of borrowing scenery, then the designs must be carefully built around this feature. It has already been pointed out that if a garden commands a particularly fine view, or if a feature of interest lies beyond the garden boundaries, it can be incorporated into the garden by careful planting and by designs that allow it to be seen above, beyond or beside the actual garden features. To do this, viewing points must be decided on and then the sight lines from it to the 'borrowed' scenery carefully worked out.

While there have always been gardens that have a view, the idea of deliberately incorporating that view into the overall design developed slowly. In the old capital, Kyoto, gardens for the rich and ruling classes were often built in the foothills of the mountains and the resulting views formed a natural backdrop. It was easy enough to arrange this by use of low walling and leaving spaces in the planting along the garden perimeter. These large suburban gardens and those actually in the city, however, soon felt the effects of an expanding population and the size of both the gardens and the views available began to shrink. So, as the cities and the number of buildings grew there was a need for designers who could make the best of such views as there were. Using new ideas and a fresh approach, it was people like Kobori Enshu who refined the art and by careful planting, that shut out the surrounding buildings but let in views of the hills, made it appear that city gardens were in fact in the country.

Thus the idea behind *shakkei* views is that boundary walls and planting should not necessarily cut off or obscure all the views from a garden, and, if a view is left open, then the design of the garden should reflect the kind of scenery it looks out on, providing a seemingly natural continuity.

So far in this chapter we have looked at what goes to make up the gardens and some of the ideas that influenced their settings, and apart from their use in the garden, it is interesting to note how some of these components came to be part of the gardening scene. Some, like the ponds, bridges and islands, date back to the very earliest gardens, some, the lanterns and water bowls, for example, originated in the old centres of worship, the Shinto shrines and early Buddhist temples, and were introduced at different times during the development of the gardens, but all came under the unifying hand of the Zen priest-gardeners who used them in their own way to create a cohesive gardening style. Although, of course, examples of the old, highly ornate temple lanterns can still be found, and gardens can still be seen that are designed on the grand style of pavilions and ponds, the advent of Zen philosophy and the way in which its followers used gardens, marked a new beginning. Size and grandiose design became unimportant beside the celebration of natural materials and humble simplicity, and it was this development perhaps more than any other, that helped make the gardens accessible to people outside Japan. If proof were needed of the popularity of these gardens amongst Western people, one has only to consider the thousands of visitors to Japan, who, every year, make visits to the gardens a central part of their stay – whether they are Zen students, garden enthusiasts or just interested onlookers. This being so, it is time now for an assessment of what these gardens can offer to the West.

In Chapter 1 and the first part of this one I have tried to pin down what the gardens actually are; the kind of gardens the Japanese make and why they make them as they do. I hope to have demonstrated that the basic difference between gardens in Japan and the West is one of approach rather than of specific differences in climate, geography, ornaments and so on, (as far as plants go, a quick look at any tree and shrub catalogue will show that a huge number of the commonest and most popular plants used in Western gardens originated in the Far East, and were introduced over here as long ago as the middle of the last century), and that it is this approach to gardening that can transcend the wide differences in eastern and western cultures. In this way the Japanese landscaping style can help create interesting alternatives for gardens in the West.

Perhaps the most important factor in this approach is the idea of a totally informal, asymmetric arrangement of features, with the rest of the garden being used as a way to pass from feature to feature. In this way the viewer is offered a number of different views and is never quite sure what he will see next. Again, rather than large vistas, the Japanese gardens depend on detail, suggestion, some surprise, and features that stimulate the imagination, catching and holding the eye. The designs offer a way of arranging rocks or features in combination with plant life that gives endless enjoyment and have a timeless quality. It is worth noting also that they tend to require less maintenance since the emphasis on dense planting, the concentration of flowers, and the lack of wide areas of grass cuts down weeding and grass cutting.

On another level Japanese designs can provide a wide range of different and new ideas for layouts and features, even if the overall garden, or the bulk of it, is to be made in a Western style. A study of the design principles detailed in Chapter 3 will provide many ideas and variations on traditional ideas. Of particular importance here is not so much the feature itself (whether it's a plant or an ornament) but the setting in which it is positioned and the angles from which it can be viewed. Concerning the rocks themselves it is important to note that Japanese gardens have always used undressed stones, taking them straight from quarries or river beds and using them in their original shape and form. In the West gardeners have traditionally used dressed stone (dressing is the processes carried out at the quarry whereby the edges of stones are evened off to give the stone one or more relatively smooth faces for building purposes), for construction work, but in recent times the price of dressed stone has become prohibitive and more and more undressed stone must be used. Thus a look at Japanese techniques for using stones can provide a variety of ideas on how they can be combined and positioned. Another design approach to be considered is the way in which Japanese gardens concentrate on individual groups, sometimes freestanding and self-contained and sometimes combined in larger schemes.

This kind of group with suitable back planting can be used in many ways: it can partially screen the front of a house from the road, divide the front garden from the back, create focal points within the garden itself, frame a view in combination with other such groups, hide unsightly objects such as compost heaps or incinerators, or break up the different parts of gardens such as beds and lawns from vegetable plots. In larger gardens where a number of such groups may be used, the basic similarities of components, rocks, shrubs, plants and screens help to give overall cohesion to the design.

But it is in the smaller areas, perhaps, that these groups and their basic design patterns have most application. For the small front garden, passageways and town gardens where the lack of space or the urban surroundings call for something a little special, the Japanese designs can provide an almost endless variety of ideas. The techniques of scaling down landscapes, the fact that the rocks can easily be laid to incorporate potted plants, and the principles of *karesansui* designing (dry arrangements that suggest the presence of water) have an application anywhere where space limits possibilities, or in the concrete and brick confines of basement areas or passageways.

As was pointed out in the first chapter, the Japanese designing techniques were created and refined over a long period of time. The small gardens of modern Japan represent the refinement of these techniques coupled with the experience of hundreds of years. They developed a kind of shorthand that made it possible to create gardens with a 'natural' feel or provide 'natural' surroundings for existing features. The designs embody the 'approach' that we have looked at in this chapter and combine it with the experience and knowledge of their history. This is the heart of what Japanese gardens can offer the West. In the garden whether it is to be entirely Japanese, or divided by groups, or if certain features, such as a view, a stream, changes of level, rocks, or particular plants or trees are to be projected and

50

developed, these Japanese designs are as relevant in the West as they are in Japan.

I have emphasized these points to illustrate how the ideas and designs can transcend the purely Japanese setting and, while retaining their distinctly Japanese feel, can be effective in the West. They are based on tradition and are guidelines or approaches rather than rules or exclusive religious concepts. The basic components of stones, rocks and the most important types of tree, shrubs and plants are all readily available in the West and need only understanding and imagination to create something new and interesting with a distinctly Japanese feel. I hope too that there is material for the enthusiast who wishes to create an entirely Japanese style garden and understand the various components. Chapter 3 details the designs and component arrangements, while Chapter 4 gives step-by-step instructions for the actual construction work.

Before going on to these chapters, however, some possible limitations concerning these designs should be taken into consideration. The most important concerns the use to which the garden will be put. As was pointed out in Chapter 1, the garden in Japan is primarily a place for relaxation and enjoyment of the presence of nature. Unlike gardens in the West they are less likely to be designed for the use of children or leisure activities. In the West, gardens are often the primary play area for children and designs have developed to cater for this with well-defined bed areas and as much lawn as possible. These are features that are not allowed for in Japanese design. A further point is the availability of specifically Japanese components. The lanterns, bowls, fencing materials and other ornaments described earlier in this chapter are, of course, produced and readily available in Japan. Apart from a limited range of them imported into the West by various companies and garden centres, many types will not be available (copies of lanterns and bowls are being produced and will be more widely available in the future). But the important thing to bear in mind is that it is not necessarily the feature or ornament itself that is essential, but the way in which it is used and highlighted. Thus there are a number of traditionally Western garden ornaments, such as sundials or bird baths that can be used in the same way with the same overall result.

Japanese designs allow for great versatility and imagination, and in the tradition of such innovators as Sen-no-Rikyu, objects can be reused for different purposes in gardens: sinks or stone pots used as water bowls, tiles and bricks reused as paths and so on. This versatility should be kept in mind and the fact that there are no rules as such as to what should be used; at the most there are guidelines as to how you can use what you have, and how you can adapt things to suit your needs. Thus if play areas are needed then the groups can be designed around these as independent units or integrated into any required design. The main point is that before any construction work is undertaken careful consideration should be given to exactly what is required of the garden and then designs drawn up to fulfil these.

3

Principles of Design

This chapter should be considered as the 'ideas' section of the book. In it are described the basic designs of, first, the component groups, and then the way in which the groups can be combined to form a variety of layouts to suit almost any need. Reading this chapter will also give an idea of the kinds of material required and a broad outline of what the various finished layouts will look like. The chapter is designed to help the reader decide whether Japanese designs are suitable for the garden and then what kind of features or groups can be included in it. As was mentioned before, the planning stage for a garden is as important as the actual construction work, since a badly planned garden, however well made, will never blend together or give the full satisfaction that comes when a carefully planned garden reaches maturity. Thus after reading this chapter attention must be given to the garden itself. What exactly is required? where? and so on. When this is clear, ideas should be taken from this chapter and either used as they stand, adapted for particular existing situations, or used in combination to achieve the required result. In addition, as mentioned in the previous chapter, thought must be given to the uses to which the garden will be put to ensure that suitable layouts are created.

Two other points should be borne in mind when reading this chapter. The first concerns the details of the designs. It is clear that all styles of gardening, whether in the East or West, include the use of stones, plants and ornaments, and it is the way that they are arranged and combined that distinguishes the many styles and different techniques. The details described in this chapter, and the guiding laws that stand behind them, are the basis of the Japanese style, and if followed carefully they will ensure that the garden, or part of the garden, will have a truly Japanese feeling. This remains true even if some non-Japanese components (alternative ornaments for example) are introduced. Thus careful attention should be paid to these details if a Japanese-style garden is required.

The second point is on a more general level. As has been pointed out in the course of the first chapter, the Japanese developed over the years a number of guidelines for construction work. They developed a kind of gardening shorthand that enabled them to reproduce aspects of the natural world on a smaller scale in the most efficient way possible. Although not specifically detailed, this shorthand is the basis of the design details; it lies behind them, guiding and supplying cohesion to the designs. Basically this shorthand has enabled them to simplify nature, pick out the most important details and bring down the scale of things to make construction possible in any-sized garden. The usefulness of this is that even if none of the designs described below are suitable for your particular garden, a careful reading of this chapter will give an understanding of the principles behind the design and this can be used to create ideas and designs of your own. This chapter is intended to yield ideas and alternatives to traditional designs in the west, and I hope it is useful to both those who wish to create a specifically Japanese garden and those who have a general interest in garden design.

1: COMPONENT GROUPS

1. *Sansui* style

We shall look first at the component groups for use in the *sansui* (mountain and water) style. This focuses on the pond (and whenever applicable streams and inlets), the mounds that provide the backdrop and additional features such as waterfalls, bridges, islands and pond edges.

Ponds
When making a garden in *sansui* style the pond should be the centre of attention. Not necessarily occupying the centre of the space available, but in any position where it provides a focal point, an overall cohesion to the design. The rest of the garden should be designed around it. Three considerations should be borne in mind when planning a pond.

The first is that the pond itself requires a focal point, a central point of interest towards which the viewers attention is focused by the features of the pond and those around it. This focal point will usually be the point at which water enters the pond, either from a stream or over a constructed waterfall. In the scheme of gardening this is the water flowing from the mountains down towards the lower land, and the focal point must be emphasized to give the impression of mountains behind. The earth mounds that form this backdrop, whatever the scale, are built up to provide support for the water inlet. The rest of the pond and the surrounding features will lead away from this point on either side.

The second consideration is that geometric symmetry should be avoided in the pond shape and its position relative to other garden features. Any number of shapes and sizes are of course possible, but anything regular or symmetric will tend to give the design a sense of formality, and therefore artificiality, that will detract from the feeling of naturalness that a Japanese garden should have.

Thirdly, it is important that the entire pond should not be clearly visible from any one spot. Its shape, with the help of careful planting, should be designed so that a number of different sight lines are available and so that each sight line offers a slightly different view. This increases the potential of the pond enormously and helps create an atmosphere of suggestion – the implication that there is much more there. Planting is of course extremely important here to ensure that each sight line is framed and that the foliage of trees or shrubs breaks up clear views of other parts of the pond.

Following these conditions, the position of the pond is important. It should, if possible, be sited so that the focal point is not immediately approachable from behind, but rather it should be visible at the far end of sight lines, creating a sense of depth and inaccessibility. Thus in Figures 10 and 11, the position of the pond in a corner (10) or against higher ground (11) means that the backdrop can effectively be built up to create the 'mountains' from which the stream is flowing. If, however, the pond is to be freestanding in a level area, then its focal point should be concentrated on an additional feature, an ornament or flowering tree for example, to give a centre to the construction (see Figure 12). Freestanding symmetric ornamental ponds are rarely found in traditional Japanese gardens, and features such as fountains never. They belong to the ornamental and geometric landscaping traditions of the West.

Given all these provisions, what shapes are suitable for pond designs? I shall look in detail at two basic, popular shapes and

Key to Figure symbols

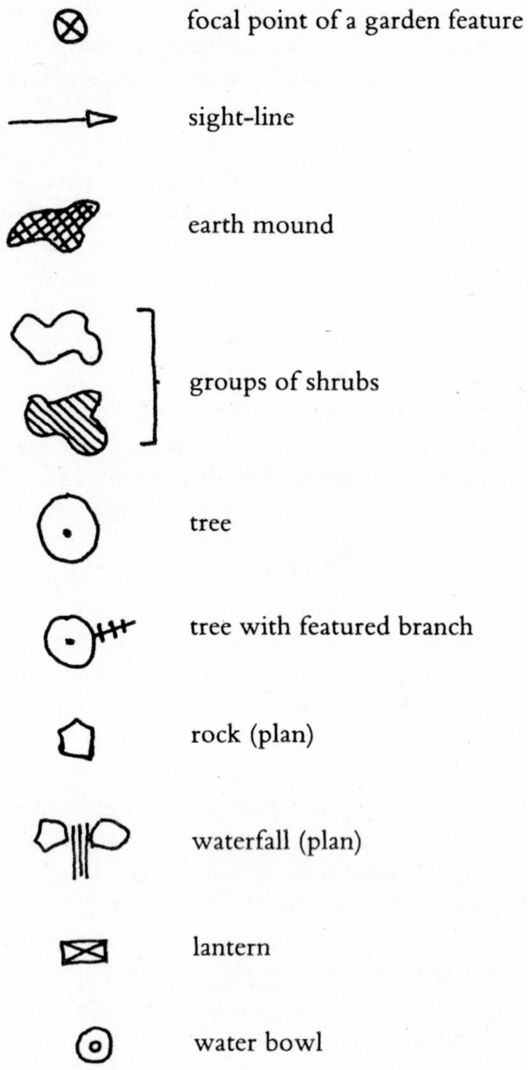

⊗   focal point of a garden feature

⟶▷   sight-line

earth mound

groups of shrubs

tree

tree with featured branch

rock (plan)

waterfall (plan)

lantern

water bowl

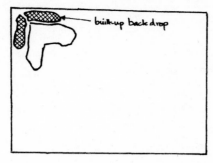

Figure 10.   Pond positioned in the corner of a garden.

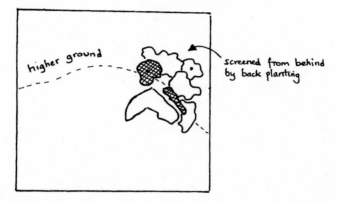

Figure 11.   Pond positioned against existing higher ground.

demonstrate how they satisfy the points above. From them a number of variations can be worked out to suit most purposes. The first is based on the heart shape and the second is a variation of an elongated figure of eight. Figures 13–16, in which the shapes are simplified for clarity, illustrate how these shapes provide first a natural focal point, second a variety of different viewing points, third a number of natural bridging positions and, generally, how they are suited for corner work. They also avoid the problems of symmetry and formality.

Figures 13a and 13b show how the focal point of either shape can be emphasized by the sympathetic addition of backing mounds. In both cases the focal point would most naturally be a waterfall of some description and the mounds heavily planted to provide depth and atmosphere.

In Figures 14a and 14b we can see how with careful planting the

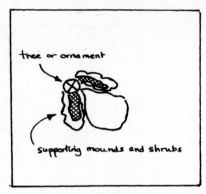

Figure 12.   Freestanding pond with added focal point.

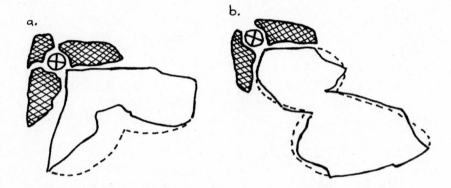

Figures 13a and b.   Basic pond shapes showing creation of focal points with backing mounds.

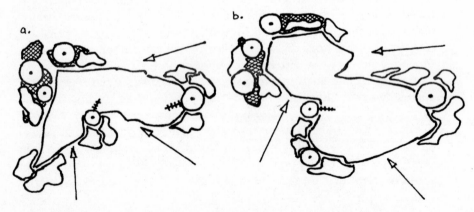

Figures 14a and b.   Creation of specific sight lines.

water and its surroundings are made visible from certain chosen sight lines (for example where paths meet the pond, or views from buildings). Ideally the focal point of the pond provides the background to each different viewpoint and the planting between the sight lines obscures other parts of the pond, making possible a variety of vistas.

Figures 15a, 15b, 16a and 16b demonstrate how versatile these basic shapes are, offering convenient bridging points and how with small alterations to the designs interesting new shapes and islands can be created. These Figures are not to any particular scale and could represent either large or small ponds. If, for example, the pond in Figure 14a is on a large scale, then the shrubs and trees would need to be of suitable size and bulk, and if smaller, dwarf bushes and smaller trees would be required.

The depth of the pond will depend on a number of factors. If the pond is to feature water plants then it will not require any great

Figures 15a and b.   Possible bridging positions.

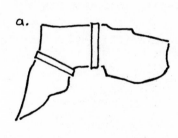
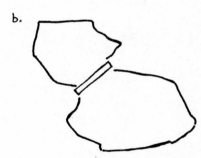

Figures 16a and b.   Variation of basic shapes to create islands.

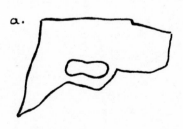
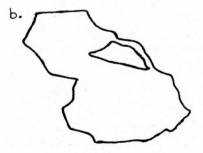

depth; if it is to contain fish then it will need to be slightly deeper. Overall, the guiding factor is that the pond provides contrast to the garden; it gives movement and sound amongst the rocks, creates reflections, and in order for it to do this effectively it needs to be as wide and deep as is practically possible. One point to remember is that it need not be uniformly deep. In this case, demonstrated in Figure 17, it should be deeper nearer the viewing points and can become shallower as it works towards the focal point. This is a useful idea that avoids the need for a lot of digging.

Waterfalls

Waterfalls are the most common focal points for ponds. They have a particular importance for the Japanese both in a symbolic sense and for good garden design. As we have seen, water, as a purifying agent, has long been a central part of Japanese spiritual life and in gardening terms the waterfalls introduce sound and movement into the design, balancing and complementing that of the wind in the trees and foliage. Whether large or small, a waterfall can generate a sense of life by its continual, everchanging splashing and gurgling.

Figure 17. Three depth stages working back from viewing point.

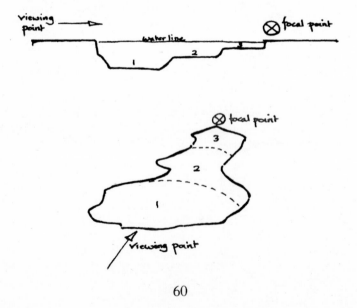

In the natural world every waterfall is different; high or low, wide or narrow, long or short, fierce or gentle, but the gardeners of old studied them closely, looked for basic similarities, and defined some fundamental characteristics. As with all other aspects of gardening, they developed a shorthand, a way to reproduce natural forms using a few guiding ideas. They studied the shapes and defined two categories, single falls and broken falls. Broken falls in turn were divided into two steps, three steps and so on. Figures 18 and 19, based on pictures from old gardening books, illustrate the simplified basic shapes. Following this, the way in which the water flowed over these shapes was noted. At its simplest this style was either smooth (Figure 20) or uneven (Figure 21) and, again, within these categories a number of subdivisions were defined; a uniformly smooth flow like a curtain (called 'cloth falling') or unevenly smooth, but not broken (called 'thread falling'). Next, the directions of the falling water was observed and three important ones decided on. In these the water fell to the left, or to the right, or in a combination of both (Figure 22). Finally the base of the fall was considered and the role of what became known as the 'water dividing stone' was defined. This stone breaks up the flow of water from the bottom of the waterfall, creating sound and more varied movement across the surface of the pond. It brings the water alive, with ripples and whirls, and rounds off the fall as a whole, completing the design (Figure 23).

It will be clear that by combining and duplicating these specified shapes, styles and directions, falls of infinite variety can be created on any required scale. Figure 24 gives an impression of how one such fall, using a combination of types, might look when planted and supported by mounds and back planting.

To construct a waterfall as shown in Figure 24, whatever scale it is done on, the most important factor is clearly the rocks used. It does not require an enormous amount of rock to build falls and create movement, only a good selection of assorted shapes and sizes. This point will be covered in detail in Chapter 4, and for the moment it is sufficient to note that not only is the size and shape of a rock important but so is its surface texture. To achieve the difference between, for example, 'cloth' and 'thread falls' (Figure 20) it is not the speed or volume of water that counts but the lip and surface of the rock over which it falls. Similarly, to create a smooth run of water (Figure 24 top right of middle section), and then slower, broken water, rocks of different texture will be needed. In terms of sound, the fall in Figure 24 will be a mixture. In general terms it will

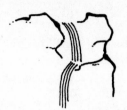

Figure 18.   Single fall.

Figure 19.   Two-step fall.
             Three-step fall.

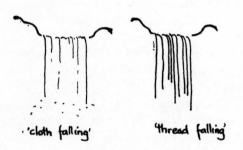

'cloth falling'   'thread falling'

Figure 20.   Smooth falls.

broken water

Figure 21.   Uneven falls.

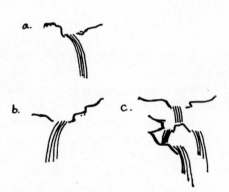

a.

b.   c.

Figure 22.   a. Right-hand fall, b.
left-hand fall, c. mixed.

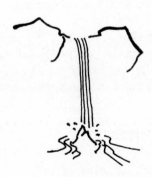

Figure 23.   Water-dividing stone.

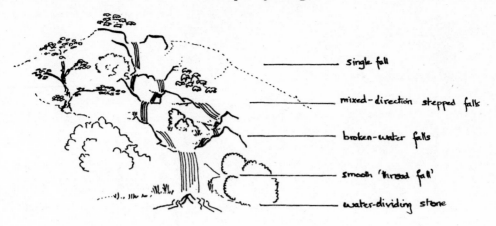

single fall

mixed-direction stepped falls

broken-water falls

smooth 'thread fall'

water-dividing stone

Figure 24.   Impression of a completed mixed fall.

feature the rush and splashes of the water passing down the middle section, and the deeper splash of the 'thread fall' into the pool. While sound is, of course, mainly a matter of chance, it is possible to introduce certain kinds. If for example, in Figure 24, a small pool were provided at the foot of the top, single fall, then deeper tones would be added to the general sound.

The final consideration concerning waterfall construction is that the sight lines across the pond should always be kept in mind while building is going on. Sight lines to the focal point should be decided on before starting work to avoid, as in Figure 25a, the angle of the fall making it almost invisible from the direction of the required sight line or, as in Figure 25b, where some of the outlying rocks cut off a view of the falls from, in this case, the right-hand side. A rough plan of the required sight lines should be made (as in Figures 14a and b) and then the fall checked from each angle as work progresses. The point to bear in mind at this stage is that each viewing angle should be presented with pleasant finished surfaces, even if not all the fall is visible (see also Appendix 1).

Bridges
As was pointed out in the second section of Chapter 1, bridges were traditionally made of a single uncut span of stone. If available, these make the most 'Japanese' form of bridge and will look good with any kind of pond.

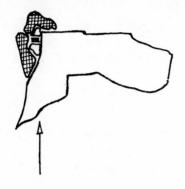 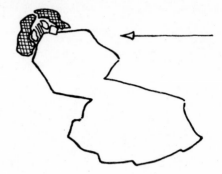

Figure 25a.   Waterfall at wrong angle   Figure 25b.   Sight line blocked by
to sight line.   outlying rock.

Nowadays, however, such pieces of natural stone are extremely hard to come by and if stone is to be used, it is usually cut to shape from larger pieces. If this still sounds expensive then it should be remembered that in demolition work and so on large flat stones such as door steps, lintels, and slate flagging are continually being broken up. It is always a good idea to check such places to see if suitable stones for a bridge are available. It is rare to find a single piece long enough to make a single span bridge, but very attractive two-span bridges can be made. Remember too, that one of Sen-no-Rikkyu's guiding tenets for materials was that old things can be used again in a new way. Figures 26 and 27 illustrate how double-span bridges might look and as Figure 27 illustrates, a bridge made of two stones of unequal thickness does not look out of place.

If stone is unobtainable, or if you prefer it, wood can be used in a number of ways. Design possibilities for wooden bridges, with either one or two spans, are limited only by the imagination, so I will only outline one or two common alternatives here to give an impression of what can be created. Figure 28a shows sawn rails laid tightly together on two supporting timbers, and a variation of this would be to use half-sawn rails although they would not have so much strength on wider bridges. Figure 28b shows the same principle using boards, which would need some kind of treatment such as creosote to help lengthen their life. An interesting variation for either a rail or a board bridge is shown in Figure 28c. A normal wooden bridge is constructed, (rails with their bark on are most suitable), and on top of this is laid a well compacted layer of thick,

Figure 26.   Double span of uncut stones.

Figure 27.   Double span of stones of unequal thickness.

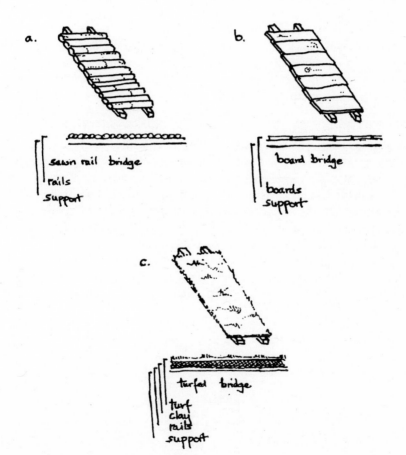

Figure 28a, b, c.   Wooden bridges.

clayey subsoil. This provides a solid, water-retaining base on which a layer of top soil and then turf is laid (details for construction are in Chapter 4, section 2). The finished effect of a grassed bridge is extremely effective, blending with the surrounding colours and textures and avoiding the harder, definite lines of cut stones or boards. Which design is most suitable depends upon the kind of effects required in the garden. Often the lines of a stone bridge serve as an excellent, eye-catching balance to the informality of the pond and rock work. This is something to be thought about during the planning stage of the work (Chapter 4, section 1).

As with stonework it should be remembered that large pieces of wood, as often as not oak, are often available at demolition sites. Large roofing timbers or wide oak floorboards can easily be converted into bridges.

As important as the materials for a bridge is its setting and associated construction. As we saw in Chapter 1, one of the most important aspects of bridge construction is that it should look well anchored. To achieve this, the ends of the bridge are locked between the 'bridge-supporting stones'. These provide bulk and solidity to the construction as well as a visual balance to the spans of the bridge. Figure 29 illustrates how these stones are placed to provide this illusion, as though they were pushing together and holding the bridge firmly. They are the base from which the bridge can spring out across the gap. These stones should be of a variety of shapes and sizes, as solid and large as possible in proportion to the bridge itself, and asymmetrically balanced with each other. Two at either end is the minimum requirement, but they may of course in turn be 'supported' by groups of stones or plants (see Figure 30).

As with everything in Japanese garden design, the points from which the bridge is to be viewed must be kept in mind. End on, as you approach it, a bridge is not particularly interesting, and so sight

Figure 29. 'Bridge-supporting stones' locking the bridge in position.

(from above)

Figure 30.   Bridge stones supported by rock groups and planting.

lines should be arranged so that the bridge can be seen, whether closely or at a distance, as it arches out over the water. In Figures 15a and 15b for example, the possible bridging positions cut across the sight lines suggested in Figures 14a and 14b, and any of them would show the bridge from an interesting angle.

Islands
Islands, like bridges, are designed to be features in the larger design of the pond. For this reason care must be taken when planning to ensure that the island when complete does not dominate the design or interrupt required views. It should be carefully constructed on the same scale as the pond and its other features. Having said this, islands can, of course, be used to alter the view across a pond and create new sight lines, directing attention to various parts of the pond. *In situ* in a pond, an island has a number of effects: it alters the scale of the whole construction and tends to emphasize the areas of water. Used carefully these qualities can enhance the design no end, but careful thought is needed to ensure that this happens.

On larger ponds, islands can be used in a more positive role. As Figures 31a and 31b indicate, islands can be positioned to create alternative focal points for the pond, thus increasing the possible viewing places. In Figure 31a the addition of the island at the opposite end of the pond to the existing focal point opens up a number of new sight lines from the left-hand side. These new lines will pass between the pond-edge planting out across the water to the island, focusing attention on the solitariness, the calm and peace of an island amidst the water, rather than on the movement and sound of the other focal point – the waterfall. Figure 31b shows similar results achieved with our other basic pond shape, and if both are carefully built to the scale of the pond, they do not intrude on the overall effect

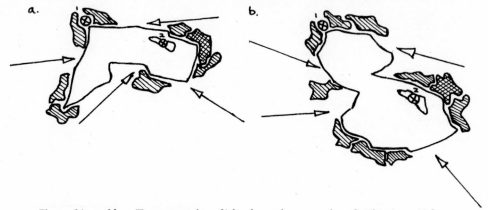

Figure 31a and b.   Two examples of islands used as secondary focal points. (Cf. Figures 14a and b.) Note additional backdrop planting or mounds behind new focal points.

of the pond feature. On small ponds, where an island may be just a single rock, the position of the island should be such that it doesn't interfere with the existing focal point. As a general rule, islands should always be planned as an integral part of the designing stage, and not added later as an afterthought.

Other possible positions for islands in the heart-shaped and figure-of-eight ponds are illustrated in Figures 32 and 33. The important point to notice is that the different island positions require different backdrop plantings and that it is the position of these that determine where the sight lines will run.

In Figure 33c the island effectively cuts the pond in half and, if planted, will create a new focal point for the lower half of the pond. This is an interesting effect since it makes a fine view in itself and gives depth to the pond, with the waterfall just visible behind it, hiding, as it were, the details of the upper half and making one want to walk round to look. All these positions will, of course, depend on whether or not there is a bridge, and should be planned with the bridge, if there is to be one, in mind. Finally, islands should not be built up too much unless they are in very large ponds. Piles of stones visible just under the surface tend to suggest too much bulk and heaviness, and will destroy the sense of depth. If possible the visible stones around the edge should run from above the surface to the bottom (as shown in Figure 34). If this is done, you will notice how this improves the scale and feeling of depth around the island.

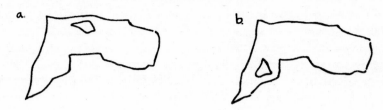

Figure 32a and b.   Alternative positions for islands in a heart-shaped pond.

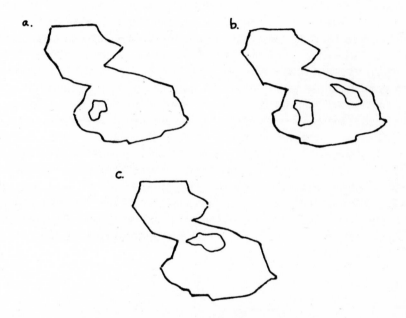

Figure 33.   Alternative positions for islands in a figure-of-eight-shaped pond.

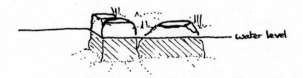

Figure 34.   Rocks at the edge of islands should reach to the bottom of pond (shaded areas are under water).

69

We will look now at the basic types of island that can be found in Japanese gardens. First the 'crane' and 'tortoise' islands that were mentioned in Chapter 2. Here the idea is to construct an island (on whatever scale is suitable) that has the overall shape and appearance of one or the other animal. This should not be taken too literally and is not as difficult as it sounds since the Japanese have developed simple, symbolic shapes for both that are easily constructed. Figure 35 shows the layout for a crane island and Figure 36 that for a tortoise (for the symbolic importance of these two see Chapter 2, p. 34). In the case of the crane the wing stone is the most important. Many of the famous crane islands in gardens in Japan feature just this one stone – a large, flat one set on edge on a supporting island; just the wing, symbolic of the crane. Extension of one end of the island to include a low line of head and neck stones develops the impression of a crane in flight, but is not essential. For the tortoise the head stone is important. It can be any oblong-shaped stone set at the correct angle, but if one with a nick, as shown in Figure 36 can be found, it should be used. (Many stones will give this shape from one angle only, and in this case the stone should be set so that the nick is visible along a major sight line.) Supporting the neck are four smaller stones placed as legs, one, slightly upturned, for the tail, and one on top to represent the baby tortoise. In both cases, realism is not really the aim. These are symbolic shapes and should not be cluttered too much with small stones and details. These 'feature' islands are particularly suitable in larger ponds for creating new focal points.

Figure 35.   Crane island. 1. The wing stone. 2. Head and neck stones.

Figure 36.   Tortoise island.
1. Head stone.
2. Leg stones.
3. Tortoise's child stone.
4. Tail stone.

Figure 37.   Two examples of rock islands.

a.   b.

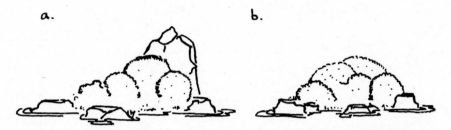

Figure 38a.   A planted island using rock and shrub features. b. Island with dense planting of flowering shrubs.

After these two, one of the most useful types of island is the single or small group of rocks. Figure 37 shows two variations of this style and as will be clear these can be tailored to suit any size of pond. The idea is that they suggest a small crag or islet, and tend to be used as an accent (giving emphasis to the water around them or a suggestion of distance) rather than being a feature in themselves.

More suitable as independent features are islands built up of rocks with a covering of soil permitting it to be planted with either a small tree, shrubs or a combination of these (Figures 38a and 38b). This style of island can also support one end of a bridge (with suitable supporting stones) and in this situation should be considered as a major part of the pond construction and not left until last or added later, since it will need secure and well-built foundations. As Figure 38a shows, islands can become excellent focal points for ponds if built away from the viewing point; the eye passes from the low stones on the front edge, up to the shrubs and then up again to the rock behind. Whatever scale this is done on, it produces a feeling of size and depth. Alternatively, the island could be thickly planted with well-shaped shrubs (azaleas, for example) that would provide a brilliant cluster of colour in the summer.

71

Figure 39a.   Chain of islets.

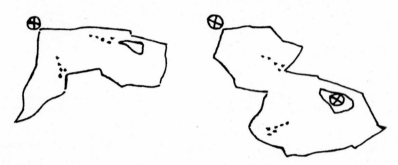

Figure 39b.   Chains of islets added to ponds to help accentuate the sight lines, leading the eye to the focal points.

It is possible that either the pond is too small to feature one of the islands described above, or large enough to require something more but not another complete island. In this case a 'chain' of islets can be used as illustrated in Figure 39a. These will comfortably fill an empty corner or can be used, by the direction in which they are laid, to accentuate or alter sight lines. Figure 39b gives some ideas on how the islets might be used. It is interesting how they too, like single rocks, can be used to suggest scale. In themselves, amongst the water and when looked at in an imaginative frame of mind they have no particular size; they could be very large or very small. This factor when used in conjunction with other features, an island or a focal point, can help create perspective and depth. To do this the pond must be completed first and then the islets added later in the required scale to produce this effect.

Whichever of these designs or positions you use, islands are fun to build and design, and, if included, will make the pond construction more interesting and rewarding to work on.

Edges
The edges of ponds, though seemingly relatively insignificant, have long been recognized by the Japanese as being an extremely import-

72

ant part of pond design. The water in the pond and the plants and trees around it are nature's own materials; they blend together without any help from us, but in a man-made situation, the point at which they meet and how they meet is of critical importance to the success of a design. It is at this point that the materials used for construction may show, and it is here too that nature's and man's materials must join together as naturally as possible. Given this, the Japanese gardeners developed a number of techniques to achieve this harmony which copy natural edges and do not interrupt the colours and textures at the pond's edge. Thus we find earth and sand edgings, pebble beaches and rocks.

It is best to avoid a uniform type of edging all the way round a pond, since this is uninteresting and lessens the possibilities for variety, and so we will look at some examples of these types of edging in combination. (The construction details for these examples are shown in Chapter 4, see pp. 120–24.) In Figure 40a, the rocks, following the line of the pond edge, frame a small pebbled beach. Beneath the pebbles the concrete skin that forms the bottom of the pond continues up until it meets the grass behind, and the pebbles

Figure 40a. Rocks and pebble beach.

Figure 40b. Rocks and sandy beach.

73

run down a short way under the water. This type of beach is most useful at points in the pond where the water is moving because it will not erode or wash away. For stiller parts of the pond the edging shown in Figure 40b can be used. Here again the concrete runs up under the sand or earth to ensure that the pond remains watertight. In either case, the rocks must be kept in proportion to the beach. This means that they should be set relatively low in the water so that they do not overpower the space between them. This is a useful rule to keep in mind on stretches of rock edging as well, since a small pond with huge rocks closing in around it will lack proportion and be spoilt visually.

If you already have a stream or natural pond in the garden that requires some kind of edging to support it or planting done near the back, then a useful material, that was widely used in the old gardens of Japan, is wooden stakes. Before concrete revolutionized garden construction, the bottoms of ponds were formed of compacted clay soil. If beaten down hard enough, it was watertight and firm enough to support rock edgings and hold stakes that were driven into it to strengthen the banks. Figure 41 shows an edge using stakes driven in close together to support a steeply sloping bank. The most suitable type of stakes are treated hardwoods, or water-resistant woods such as alder, if this is available. Whatever kind of edgings you use, be sure to plan them at the same time as the pond itself so that you know where your rocky cliffs or pebbled beaches will be. Beaches, being lower openings to the pond, if carefully framed by rocks or plants make excellent starting places for sight lines.

Figure 41.   Wooden stakes supporting a steep bank.

Karesansui style

Designing for *karesansui* gardens (dry landscapes) should be tackled in exactly the same way as has been detailed above. The same considerations should be kept in mind and the same principles for design should guide the work. Everything will be the same, including sight lines, positionings, proportions and so on, except that the waterfall will be dry and the pond will consist of a grass or gravel

Figure 42.   *Karesansui*-style garden with grass.

Figure 43.   *Karesansui*-style garden with gravel.

75

surface. This may sound odd, but it is surprising how much movement and interest can be created with this method. After all, the important design points are still present: the contrast of a large, flat area amongst the jumble of rock and foliage, the possibilities of differing views and the creation of a feature that stands out in the garden. A dry pond with its surface of closely cut grass, or neatly raked gravel or stones, complete with bridges, islands and edges can be every bit as exciting and rewarding as one containing water, and requires considerably less work.

After the design of the pond has been finalized, a shallow depression is dug in the shape of the pond, the islands, bridges and edges set on the dry solid earth and then the surface material is spread or laid to cover the bottom. If done properly it requires only the smallest effort of imagination to bring this 'pond' to life.

Figures 42 and 43 illustrate a pond finished with two different materials. In Figure 42 grass is used as the surface and all the details of an ordinary pond are visible. The waterfall stones forming the focal point complete with back drop and water-dividing stones. Edgings of stakes and rocks lead away round the pond. The bridge, with all the correct construction details provides access to a small island, with a rock feature and a covering of small shrubs. The island stands in the grass in the same way as it would in water with the edging stones not too far above the surface. Figure 43 shows the same pond using gravel. Here it is important to notice how the surface of the gravel can be raked in lines to suggest the movement of water. In another sense, the gravel suggests that the pond is only temporarily dry, and that after rain the pond will fill with water. Many of the most famous gardens in Japan feature gravel used in this way.

It is not always practical or desirable to use water itself in a pond but this should not mean that the idea of pond should be discounted entirely. With a little imagination and good planning it is surprising what can be achieved.

3. Rock groups

As will now be apparent to anyone who has read the preceding sections of this chapter and studied the illustrations, rocks, on their own or in groups, feature in every part of the garden. In Chapter 1 we looked at the basic shapes of rock identified by the old gardeners and at some of the reasons behind the groups they constructed. In this section, we will analyse how grouping rocks should be approached first for the creation of a specific rock feature, and then for more general use such as edgings.

The key point to remember in any work concerning rocks is balance. Not the symmetrical balance of the classic European gardens such as Versailles or Blenheim where square beds and parallel paths balance out in a general scheme, but the implicit, asymmetrical balance of shapes and patterns that we have met time and time again throughout this book; the balance of colours and textures, water and foliage, blank spaces and details, even in the arrangement of tea utensils. It is in fact one of the basic ideas behind the Japanese approach to gardening. So, how does this balance work out in rock groupings?

The sequence of work illustrated in Figures 44a–e shows one example of how a rocky feature may be constructed. In Figure 44a the central stone of the group is set. It is the stone which will catch the eye at a distance and forms the basis of the group. Since the first stone is of a tall, thin type, the second, a short, squat stone (Figure 44b) is used to anchor the first and give width to the group. In Figure 44c, a low flat stone is used in front of the group to lead the eye in, to balance the vertical height of stone 1., and create space in front of the group. Next, on the left, an arched stone is used to balance stone 2., while its shape leads the eye towards the top of the central stone (Figure 44d). A final stone is added (Figure 44e) to fill out the group, and by its additional bulk on the left, balance the spreading away to the bottom right.

Two points should be noted about this sequence. First there are clearly any number of combinations in which these five stones could be arranged. The sequence shown here is only an example of how groups should be systematically built up, using an assortment of the basic stone shapes to create an inner balance within the group. Before deciding on a definite grouping for your feature it is advisable, and fun, to experiment with a number of combinations, plot them on paper for reference, and later choose the one you think is most suited to the particular situation or which you like best. The guidelines do not determine where particular stone shapes should stand in relation to another, only what the final result should try to achieve: balance and cohesion. The second point is that a feature can consist of as many or as few stones as you like. In the sequence shown in Figure 44 work could stop after two stones, three stones and so on, since each stone should be placed in such a way that the group is

a.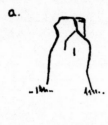

b.

c.

d.

e.

Figure 44. Construction of a rock feature.
a. Tall, thin stone.
b. Short, squat stone added.
c. Flat stone placed in front.
d. Arched stone added on the left.
e. Group filled out with additional bulk on left.

self-contained yet capable of expansion if required. There is room for plenty of experimenting.

Figure 45 shows two slight variations of style which should be noted. Here, smaller groups are balanced at a slight distance by stones placed in such a way that they can either be seen as independent units or as part of a larger, more spacious group (Figure 45a and b). It will be noticed that these stones can play a similar role to that of the chains of islets in ponds: they can accentuate sight lines and lead the eye in certain directions.

This balancing at a distance is also the key to the successful use of rocks as edgings. As has been pointed out with reference to the amount of rock that shows above water, rocks should not appear too dense and massive, since this tends to crowd and overpower the setting.

Figure 45. Different styles of rock group.

An example of rock balancing around the focal point is shown in Figure 46 where large feature stones, placed at a distance on the left and right, while being features in themselves, also give the composition of the waterfall larger scope and more depth. They also help to provide cohesion to the whole area around the focal point, framing it and providing perspective. Figures 47a and b, illustrate in plan how four or five large feature stones could be used around a pond, the edging in between them being a suitable mixture of smaller rocks, beaches and pebbles. A quick look back at Figure 42 may help to illustrate how these rock groupings fit into a finished scene.

The rock grouping (Figure 42) of the dry waterfall is fairly large and solid. Therefore, movement and a counterbalancing bulk is established by a quick succession of smaller, more mixed rock shapes that lead away to the right. They terminate in a large feature stone that in one sense completes the waterfall and in another frames the left-hand side of the next feature, the pebble beach. (On the left of the waterfall, heavy planting is used partly to screen the fall, suggesting more detail behind, and partly to balance the line of rocks

Figure 46.   Example of rocks balanced round the focal point.

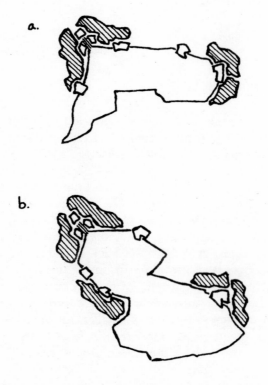

Figure 47.   Two plans illustrating possible sites for major feature stones.

The golden pavilion at Kinkaku-ji (Kyoto) overlooks a wide pond designed in the Pure-Land tradition, big enough for boating. Note in particular the designs of the two island groups; in the foreground is an example of a crane island, with its large wing stone, while in the middle distance lies a tortoise island. Both were used to symbolize long life and good health.

Japan National Tourist Organization

Left: This corner of the Imperial Palace garden at Shugaku-in (Kyoto) illustrates how the various components of water, rock and plants were blended together. Attention is focused on the feature rocks beside the water, and then the eye is led away over the bridge and up the path. Well-trimmed shrubs provide the backdrop. *William MacQuitty*

Below: At Katsura Villa (Kyoto) the strong lines of the bridges are complemented and offset by the use of tall, upright bridge-supporting stones. These not only fill out the individual groups but also link up with the lantern feature in the foreground, giving the whole layout an overall cohesion. *William MacQuitty*

Right: Soseki's garden at Saiho-ji (Kyoto) marks the transitional period between the Pure-Land gardens and those of the Zen priests. Here a large pond has been filled in with islands to create an intricate layout of waterways. With these changes the garden took on a much more personal and secluded atmosphere; more mysterious and imaginative. *William MacQuitty*

Below: This picture of the garden at Katsura Villa (Kyoto) illustrates how focal points can be used. Looking along this sight line, attention is directed towards the lantern feature. Rocks define the view on the left, and careful planting screens the rest of the garden away to the right. *William MacQuitty*

Left: This detail of the pond at Tenryu-ji (Kyoto) shows how a combination of components can be used along the edges. Note the use of large feature stones to lead the eye round the pond. *Japan National Tourist Organization*

Below: The stone garden at Ryoan-ji (Kyoto) is probably the best known Zen garden in Japan, and its effect is achieved without plants or water. The imagination is set free. *William MacQuitty*

Above: A corner of the garden at Zuiho-ji (Kyoto). Here the designers have used back-planting and slightly raised ground as a setting for the rock gravel feature. *J. Allan Cash Library*

The natural progression from tile to pebbles, to gravel leads the eye out into the garden at Tofuku-ji (Kyoto). *Japan National Tourist Organization*

These three photographs illustrate how the gravel surfaces of Zen gardens can be used as design features in their own right. Occasionally priests change the patterns to help stimulate their students.

Above: The gravel has been raked in long, wavy lines to make it stand out dramatically from the straight lines of the surrounding buildings.
Sean Sprague

Opposite above: Here two small mounds have been raised, altering the whole perspective of the otherwise flat space. *William MacQuitty*

Opposite below: Groups of meticulously laid concentric circles bring this garden alive with the movement of rain drops rippling the surface of a pond and of water lapping round the stones along the edges. This is an excellent example of what can be achieved with *karesansui* designs.
Japan National Tourist Organization

Above: The completed waterfall at Hakujuso (Osaka). The water falls from the header pool behind stone 6, in a curtain fall onto stone 5, over the irregular lip of this in a more broken fall onto stone 1, whence it slides down into the pond. The jumble of stones in front of the fall are waiting to be positioned around the edges of the pond. *A. K. Davidson*

Below: The fall at Hakujuso in general perspective. Stone 11 can now be seen in its role as bridge-supporting stone, and the low flat stone to the right of the fall is ready to receive a lantern. The whole fall has been rounded off by careful planting of a black pine behind stone 12. *A. K. Davidson*

on the right.) In a wider view, the eye is lead from the fall, to the feature stone on the right, from here to the bridge-supporting stone, across the bridge to the large stone on the island, and from here back up to the fall, creating a complete, balanced and changing scene. (See also Appendix 1, p. 141, for balance in waterfall groups.)

Finally, before we leave rocks, a note about different types. Inevitably, you will have to use whatever kind of rock is available and not too expensive in your area whether they are from beaches, rivers or lakes, mountains or dug from quarries. Generally speaking, though, sedimentary type rocks will lend immediate authenticity to the scene, with their weathered faces worn by water or time and the elements. On the other hand metamorphic rocks, produced by the enormous pressures underground, feature beautiful strata patterns and wide ranges of colours, making them particularly suitable for featured stones. Rock types should not be mixed too much since this will look unnatural but with care they can all be blended together.

The aim of this section has been to give a general impression of how rocks can be used. Using the guidelines set down here and your own ideas a wide variety of rock groups can be created. Your eye will tell you whether you have achieved the correct balances within the design.

4. Ornaments

In Chapter 1 we looked in detail at the origins of the important types of ornament and suggested why they came to be used in gardens. In this section we are going to study the settings and positions for them in the garden. As with most components in a Japanese garden, they do not stand alone, isolated or unsupported. Just as the focal point of a pond needs a backdrop, so the ornaments require support from various stones, and care must be taken concerning their position in the garden. The two major ornaments, lanterns and bowls, both have a formalized arrangement of stones to make up the surrounding groups and traditionally, these stones, as we shall see, had specific uses. There are also instances when lanterns can be used as part of the group around a waterbowl creating some very interesting features.

Lanterns
Although in modern times lanterns may well contain electric light bulbs or remain unlit, being used for decorative purposes only, they originally contained a tallow candle which required lighting by hand

from another candle or burning torch. Thus a minimum of two stones placed around the lantern were required; one to stand on and one to receive the container in which the candle or torch was carried. These were the 'lamp-lighting stones' and, even if not used today, they have become part of the design. Figure 48 gives an example of how these stones might be grouped around a lantern. As can be seen from the drawing, a large flat stone is placed in front of the lamp and a slightly higher, bulkier stone set next to it. The former represents the stone that would have been stood on and the latter the place for the basket or bowl used to carry the taper. The size of the stones will depend to a certain extent on the height and bulk of the lantern, aiming to keep the group in proportion. In turn, the size of lantern should be in proportion with the section of garden in which it stands; a four- or five-foot lantern set amongst a small-scale waterfall and pond design will clearly destroy the sense of scale that is so important for the success of the pond. In the West, wrought-iron carriage lamps on pedestals or home-made wooden ones should be considered if stone lanterns are not available. (Note, however, that leading nurseries and garden centres often have stone lanterns; it is worth finding out if they are available locally.)

Next to the group itself, its location is important, and Figure 49 indicates some of the more obvious positions for a lantern. These are places where a lantern would logically be placed if it were to be used and this is important since it suggests that the lantern has a theoretical purpose and is not placed at random for purely decorative purposes. This is in keeping with the spirit of Japanese gardening that, as mentioned in Chapter 1, excludes decoration for its own sake.

In Figure 49, four principle sites for lanterns are shown. Number 1. is positioned next to an entrance to the garden, and whether this is

Figure 48.   Lantern with lamp-lighting stones and back planting.

(plan)

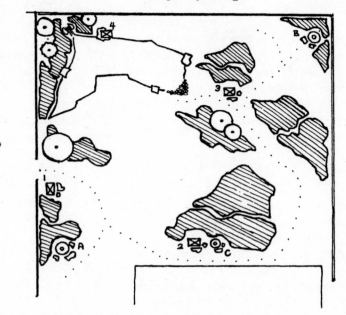

Figure 49. Principle sites for lantern groups and water bowls.

a main gate or a smaller side wicket, a lantern could well be used here to light the gateway and path leading from it. This is also a useful place in the sense that it catches the eye immediately setting the tone of the garden and giving the visitor an early glimpse of what is to be expected. Number 2. serves a similar purpose from its position close to the house, where it could light the way from the house into the garden. If positioned in close view of a window and supported by planting, it will also make a very pleasant feature visible from indoors.

Number 3. is an example of a lantern group placed at a point where paths join, an extension of the traditional use of lanterns at crossroads in ancient Japan. In an average-sized garden one or two should be the maximum number used and these should be placed at the larger intersections. To use more would clutter up the garden and detract from their effect. Using a lantern in this position means that it can also form the focal point in the scene towards which you are walking. In the case of Figure 49, the lantern would, for example, form the focal point as you walked up the right-hand side of the garden from the house. Reaching it he pond would become visible clearly and another view and focal point would take over. Lantern number 4. is positioned on a feature stone near the focal point of the

83

pond, and becomes part of the overall scene. In this case it should be a small, low one so that it does not dominate its surroundings. In a garden today, if any of the lanterns are to be working, this might be the one to choose. If it is, it should not be too bright, giving just a gentle, mellow light, and at night it will transform the scene. This can be a particularly beautiful effect if one light in the garden creates a glow that picks out the movement of the waterfall and the ripples across the pond. It is an effect that is well worth the extra work. ❦

Water bowls

Water bowls, like lanterns, were originally functional and so, in the same way as lanterns, they require a group of stones around them for use when washing or filling the bowl. This is true whether the bowl is a tall, cut-stone *chōzubachi*, or a lower, natural stone *tsukubai*. Basically, the bowls require a stone in front for standing on, a stone to the right for putting the water container on, and one to the left for standing a portable lantern on. The other integral part of the group design is a drain for used or excess water to soak away into. Figure 50 details a typical group in plan, section and then elevation. In this example, the group is centred around a *tsukubai*. The group would be filled out after completion with back planting.

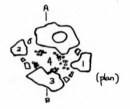

Figure 50. Stone group around water bowl.
1. Water-container stone.
2. Lantern stone.
3. Standing stone.
4. Water drain.

earth cut away to form
the water drain

84

Figure 51.   Water-blow group supported by lantern, feature stone and back planting. Note dipper laid across the bowl when not in use.

Figure 51 shows how a bowl group might be combined with a larger stone lantern, and reference back to Figure 49 will show some typical positions for bowl groups. As will be clear from this drawing, water bowls A and B are used as features in their own right, being a useful item to fill odd corners of the garden. Bowl C is used in conjunction with a lantern to make an interesting group in front of the house.

In the West the large, rather formal *chōzubachi* may be rather hard to come by, but any stone with a suitable depression can be used in *tsukubai* styles since they do not need to be deep and can be of any shape. There are also a number of common objects such as stone urns, old troughs or large jars that could also be used, providing they are interesting to look at and generally blend with the colours of the surrounding rocks and plants. Similarly, dippers need not be of bamboo, and as long as they can scoop up water, could be anything that will suit the setting. (Figure 51 shows the position in which a dipper is usually kept on the water bowl.)

Stupa and *sozu*

The *stupa* (stone memorial towers) are perhaps the most exclusively Eastern of the garden ornaments covered here, and for this reason are unlikely to be readily available in the West in any shape or size. They are, however, an important part of many gardens in Japan and add considerably to the atmosphere, contributing a kind of mysteriousness. They can be used almost anywhere in a design where a feature or a new focal point is required and the important point to note about their positioning is that they should not stand out too strongly. Ideally a *stupa* will be nestled amongst foliage, so that it is glimpsed rather than seen, and in most gardens they will have a branch of a tree trained across in part of them to help break up the lines and add to the feeling of suggested detail (see Figure 52). Not more than one should be used unless the garden is very big.

Use of a *sozu* (bamboo dipper) will depend to some extent on the scale of the garden. For it to have any real effect, the barrel will need to be 1ft 6in to 2ft long, and this will make it too large for small designs. It must also be fed from above which means that it will need to be situated near a change in ground level (i.e. where a small waterfall might have been) and this again may cause difficulties in a small garden. If, however, the garden is large enough to take one, constructing and installing a *sozu* (see Chapter 4) should be considered since it represents something specifically Japanese and will subsequently be a point of interest.

Finally, let me add an additional note of warning concerning the use of ornaments. They should be used sparingly, for maximum effect, and not situated in overly contrived positions. The idea to be kept in mind is that an ornament and its supporting stones should be more or less out of sight until one comes across them while walking round the garden. They should come as something of a surprise, something out of the ordinary, and the visitor should not be aware of them all the time. Perhaps this is a suitable place to quote a remark made by one of the great Japanese *shoguns* Tokugawa Ieyasu who noted that 'the insufficient is better than the superfluous'. He is referring to art and design in general, but it applies very aptly to the use of ornaments and should be kept in mind while filling out the details of a garden design.

We shall turn now from the components that make up the features in the garden to those which make the overall designs possible: the components which join up the various groups that we have created and give cohesion to the ideas. Included here are the paths which take one to different parts of the gardens, opening up the various sight lines and taking us past the varied places of interest. Then we have

Figure 52.   *Stupa* situated in dense foliage.

the walls, fences and screens that form the background to the focal points, plants and ornaments, divide them from each other and create the different 'spaces' within the garden.

5. Paths

Paths can generally be divided into two distinct sorts: stepping-stone paths and continual unbroken ones. Which is used depends on materials available, personal taste and the degree of formality that is desired. Broadly speaking, stepping-stone paths of well-weathered stones set amongst the moss or grass ground covering are the most common and informal type of path. They have none of the bulk and straight lines of a continual path and blend in easily with the shapes and colours of the garden around. Continual, decorative paths, however, have their role. If required, they can lend a sense of balance to the informality of the plant and rock arrangements. They also provide a route and access for wheelbarrows and are more useful for maintenance work. The ideal overall design may be of the type shown in Figure 53 where continual paths of different designs provide access to the various parts of the garden, and stepping-stone paths lead off to the various features: the highways and the byways.

Figure 53.   Diagram illustrating use of solid paths to provide access to the different parts of the garden, with stepping-stone paths to the various features. Note also use of terrace in front of house and the variety of path-surface designs.

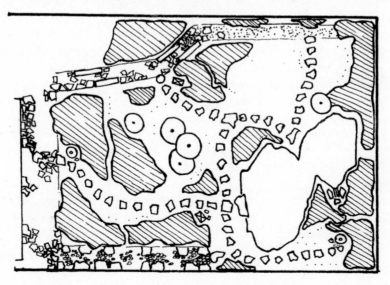

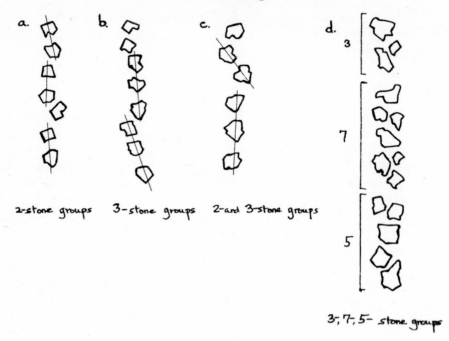

2-stone groups   3-stone groups   2-and 3-stone groups

3,7,5- stone groups

Figure 54.   Stones grouped in twos, threes, etc.

We will look first at some designs for stepping-stone paths. Working on the basis that straight paths of equally spaced stones look both unnatural and are uninteresting, the Japanese defined a number of basic groupings in which stones could be laid. Figures 54a–d illustrate some of these for use with traditionally shaped stepping-stones (i.e. generally flat and round stones).

As can be seen from these drawings, stones are grouped in twos, threes, and so on, and these groups are used to break up the symmetry of the path. In Figures 54a and b, the groups of two and three are laid at slightly different angles to each other, even though the path continues in the same direction, resulting in a pleasantly broken-up effect that nevertheless has some kind of rhythm and cohesion. Figure 54c shows an example of how the numbers can be mixed with similar results and Figure 54d shows how the numbers three-five-seven (see Chapter 2, p. 36) can be employed to make up a very pleasant path.

Over long lengths of path these basic units could be repeated or mixed together according to personal taste.

An alternative to planning a path by groups is to decide on an overall set pattern for the whole length of the path, in which case the rhythm provided by the smaller groupings is replaced by a larger rhythm running through the whole path. Figures 55a, b and c give examples of how this can be achieved.

Figure 55a shows single stones, irregularly spaced around a long sweeping curve. In use, the whole of this curve may not be visible at one time but walking around we will become conscious of it, and this gives the path an overall sense of design, which may not be apparent at any given point but of which the user slowly becomes aware. Figures 55b and c show alternative methods of achieving this overall design and are based on different-sized zigzag patterns. It is interesting to note here the Japanese names for the designs shown in these two figures, since it illustrates something of their approach to gardening. In the West we might call these, as I have done, large or small zigzags, but in Japan they are seen as interpretations of natural phenomena and named accordingly. Thus the style in Figure 55b is known as *gan-kake* (literally meaning 'wild-geese' style) and Figure 55c as *chidori-kake* (literally 'plover' style). The reason is not hard to find if you look at the styles as though they represented the different flight patterns of the two birds. The geese have a relaxed, flowing flight using long, slow wing beats, while the plover's flight is altogether quicker and more darting. The larger point to be made

Figure 55. Different path designs: a. 'curving design', b. 'wild-geese' design, c. 'plover' design.

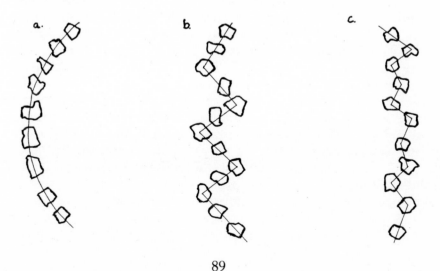

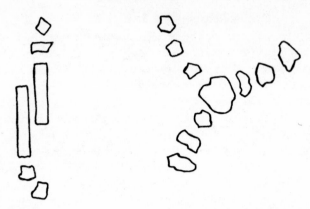

Figure 56. 'Poem-card' path.   Figure 57.   Path-dividing stone.

here is that this is part and parcel of the different approach to gardening that we have seen as being one of the basic differences between Japanese and Western gardening styles, and around which the unique Japanese style has evolved.

Paths need not, of course, be made up entirely of one type of basic stone shape, and many interesting designs can result from a mixture. Figure 56 shows how rectangular slabs can be grouped in one of two places in an otherwise standard stepping-stone path. This technique leads to some interesting contrasts and could be used as a self-contained feature at a point, for example, where the path is passing through thick planting and no other feature or specific sight line is in view. The style illustrated in Figure 56 is known as a 'poem-card' style since the stone shapes are similar to the small pieces of card on which poems are written and hung on trees during various festivals.

One of the most important stones in a network of paths is the path-dividing stone (Figure 57). This stone is placed at junctions, and it should be slightly larger than those around it to emphasize and act as a kind of visual fulcrum for the paths radiating from it. In many gardens, this stone becomes a feature in itself since stones from old temples or other buildings are often used. In the West there are a number of stones suitable for use as a path divider, such as disused mill stones or the patterned base of an old cheese press. Whatever kind of stone is used, the path-dividing stone should stand out amongst the others and accentuate the meeting point of the paths.

A point should be made here concerning the way in which stones should be laid in these stepping-stone paths. Unless the stones are

90

perfectly round they should, as a general rule, be laid across the width of the path and in such a way that the sides are not quite parallel with the next. Figure 58 illustrates how this works. The stones are laid sideways which gives an impression of width and solidity, rather than lengthways (which makes the path look narrow and less inviting) and the edges are at any angle to each other. This helps avoid unwanted symmetry and makes the path more informal and varied.

Before passing on to continuous types of path, it should be remembered that stepping stones can, of course, also be used for their original purpose as a way of continuing a path across a stretch of water, and in any pond this is a useful alternative to constructing bridges. If used in this way the same principles of design as detailed above apply, with the additional note that on small ponds, the stones should be kept as low in the water as possible to prevent them from overwhelming the design.

The other main kind of path design is to have a continual, unbroken kind of surface and these, as we saw in the introduction to this section, are used mainly for access and maintenance around the garden, and often in front of the house acting as a kind of terrace (see Figure 53). On the whole the Japanese tend to favour a mixture of components for the surface since to some extent this breaks up the lines of the path and gives it a variety of textures and colours. One popular design of this type is shown in Figure 59 where flagstones

Figure 58.   Position of stones in relation to each other: long edges not parallel and laid across the width of the path.

Figure 59.   Flagstone and pebble design.

are mixed with smaller pebbles. In Figure 60 the flatter surfaces of poem cards and crazy paving are matched, while in Figure 61 the large, flat shapes of the concrete slabs (preferably the non-vibrated type, see Chapter 4) are contrasted with the small round shapes of pebbles. In this design colour and shapes play a role. Figure 62 gives an idea of how ordinary crazy paving, using whatever broken material may be available, might be laid and Figure 63 illustrates one of the many patterns that can be made with bricks. Crazy paving is always a useful and versatile path surface since the pieces can be of any shape, size or material. Bricks, although rather expensive to buy new these days, are a very popular medium in the West already and they are well known for the lovely colours and textures that they take on when weathered and covered by moss. Second-hand bricks may be available, it is always worth checking locally. Finally, we have gravel paths. Using gravel has a number of distinct advantages, the most immediate of which are that it is cheap, available almost anywhere and probably the easiest type of path to lay. In addition to this is the very pleasant sound produced when walking over it, and it is this factor that has made gravel one of the most widely used materials in Japanese gardens, temples and shrines. On the whole these considerations considerably outweigh the main disadvantage of gravel which is that it needs periodic attention in the form of weeding and smoothing out.

As with stepping-stone paths the main point to remember is that over the whole garden a number of designs can be used to add interest and variety (Figure 53) providing that they are not overdone, in which case the result might be confusing and distracting. One additional point to be made is that paths provide an important link between the house and the garden. In the example shown in Figure 53 the use of crazy paving in front of the house and on the sections of path leading away from it provides a useful visual link between the viewing point (door or window) and the garden immediately visible from it. This technique helps draw the eye, and with it the viewer's interest, out into the garden. This is an important aspect of successful design that should be kept in mind during the planning stage.

6. Walls, fences and screens

The last group of garden components to be looked at in this section are the walls, fences and screens that will be used to surround and divide up the garden. In fact there are three important and different

Figure 60.   'Poem cards' and crazy paving.

Figure 61.   Concrete slabs and pebbles.

Figure 62.   Crazy paving.

Figure 63.   A brick pattern.

functions to be identified here. First, the boundary of the garden requires a wall or fence that will help cut it off from its immediate surroundings, to help build up the calm, quiet type of atmosphere that is suitable for this type of garden. The only exception here would be a garden that includes a 'borrowed' (*shakkei*) view, in which case a section of the wall would be left out. Secondly, there are the internal screens, structures which break up the garden and often act as backdrops for a particular feature group. On the whole these will be solid (in the sense that they cannot be seen through) and are often used to screen off the different views or hide unwanted parts of buildings or the garden. Finally the fences: low, lightweight structures which do not actually break up the view, but which suggest spaces and emphasize the parts between them. These differences will, I hope, become clear as well look at each type in more detail.

Work done on the boundaries of the garden is likely to be the most permanent and therefore involves more planning and thought. As has been mentioned, the garden will need to be cut off as much as possible from whatever surrounds it. The first job therefore is to decide what is to be cut out and what, if anything, is to be included in the garden design. Having done this the degree of cutting off required must be decided on. If, for example, there are buildings close to the boundary, then a combination of walls and high, dense planting will be required. If there is a busy road nearby then less height will be needed but thick planting to reduce the noise will be necessary. On the other hand, if there are things at a slight distance to be shut out then probably a good wall will suffice. These points are important not just from the point of view of privacy but also to ensure that the garden takes on the right, secluded atmosphere.

Let us look now at how these varying degrees of screening can be achieved using stone walls and planting. Figure 64 shows the cross section of an arrangement for maximum screening where buildings close to the garden present a problem. In the drawing it will be seen that the combination of a good, solid wall, tall planting beside it and then dense shrubs inside that, build up to the necessary depth to cut out the building and, at the same time, hide the actual boundary from the garden side. This can be an important factor in smaller gardens where the feeling of size is increased if the garden appears to continue back past the planting. Using stone walls has one distinct advantage over fences and hedges which is that soil can be built up against them, permitting the kind of arrangement shown in Figure 65. Here the boundary wall also supports the backdrop for a waterfall and at the same time reduces the height of trees and shrubs required. The screening effect of the arrangement is undiminished.

Figure 64.   Boundary wall and back-up planting.

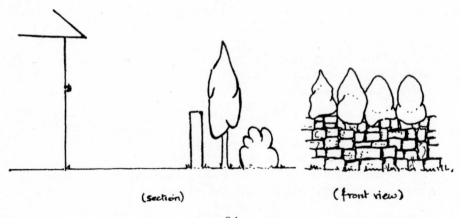

(section)   (front view)

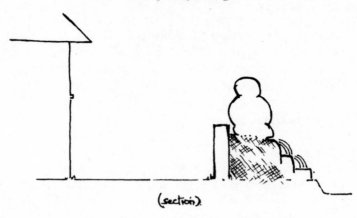

(section)

Figure 65.   Boundary wall supporting earth mound for waterfall.

Other materials that can be used on boundaries include fences, such as lapped panels, and hedges. Panels have the advantage of being quick and easy to erect and are cheaper than any other material that does the same job. They are not, however, suitable for supporting either earth or climbing plants, but apart from this they can be used in much the same way as stone walls as is illustrated in Figure 66.

With these factors in mind, perhaps the best idea for gardens that require screening all round would be a combination of walls and

Figure 66.   Boundary fence (lapped panels) and back-up planting.

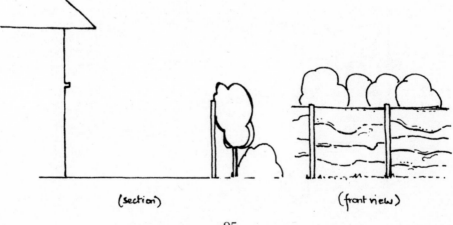

(section)   (front view)

panel-type fencing or good, stout hedging. An example of this is shown in Figure 67, and it will be noticed how walls are used where built-up earth is required and panels on the other sections. Allowance has also been made for a *shakkei* view, with a lower section of fence used at the point where the sight line meets the boundary. This gap is then framed on either side by trees or large shrubs to focus attention on the featured view.

Internal fences and screens

As important as the boundaries of the garden is the way in which a garden is divided up internally. In many gardens the positioning and density of the planting will, to a large extent, separate one part of a garden from another. An example of this can be seen in Figure 53. Here, the thickly planted groups of shrubs serve to break up the overall shape of the garden and create specific spaces within it. As we have seen before, this is one of the fundamental design principles for Japanese gardens, whereby the paths lead the viewer round the garden from one scene to another, while each viewing point offers something different and new.

Figure 67. Use of walls and fencing for the garden boundary. Note the wall supporting the backing mounds for the pond and the gap in the trees for sight line to view beyond.

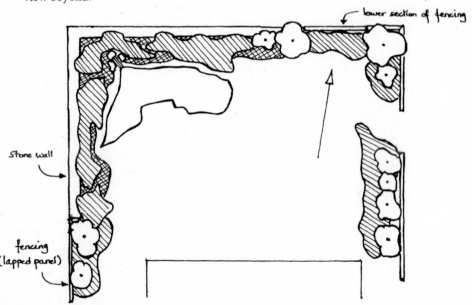

lower section of fencing

Stone wall

fencing
(lapped panels)

Figure 68.   Lapped-panel screen
forming backdrop for a water bowl.   Figure 69.   Bamboo screen.

This is the most informal method of dividing up a garden, relying as it does on the size and density of the shrubs, and the next step is to introduce screens or longer stretches of fences or hedges to provide additional emphasis and definition to the shapes and features. Screens, in this context being short lengths of 'fence' that form the backdrop to a particular feature or focal point, and longer fences, can be of two types. They can either be solid, in that they block the view entirely, or they can be see-through, creating a barrier, while not actually blocking the view beyond.

Solid screens and fences can be made of a number of materials, perhaps the most convenient of which would be lapped panels. Figure 68 illustrates this type of material in use as the backdrop for a water-bowl group. This has the effect of concentrating attention on the bowl and forming a well-defined focal point (see Figure 74 for possible positions). Apart from the other advantages mentioned above, panels are also very versatile and when combined in long lengths are a useful way to separate the different areas, such as car park, garden and sheds. This is particularly true in a garden where only a part is made in the Japanese style, and where this needs to be divided from the rest.

Another important material for screens or fences is bamboo, and there are a number of ways in which this can be used. Figure 69 shows bamboo used in a similar situation as the lapped panels, and here the very presence of bamboo helps to create a specifically Japanese feeling. This, plus its versatility, is the main advantage of using bamboo. Once you have the bamboo poles, either whole or sawn in half lengthways, a number of interesting designs can easily be created. Figures 70–72 illustrate how bamboo can be used to make lightweight, see-through screens or fences, that can be used in a number of ways to define spaces within the garden, concentrating attention on certain features, without actually blocking off the view.

This use of screens is, as we have seen, useful for creating the right kind of garden layout and helps ensure, in conjunction with the shrub groups, that not too much of the garden is visible at a time. It helps create an air of suggestion and of surprises in store. The degree to which this technique is used will depend upon personal taste, but using some bamboo screening is a useful way to emphasize the 'Japanese' nature of the garden.

The designs illustrated in Figures 70–72 show some of the more popular patterns and a number of variations are, of course, possible. The things to notice are, first, that these can be of any required height and used as single short lengths for screens or extended into longer fences. These considerations will depend on the actual situation and its requirements. The second point, illustrated in Figure 71, is that the shape need not be square and regular, but can be varied in a number of ways. The sloping shape shown here is found in most of the old gardens in Japan either for single, backdrop screens, or on the end of fences, giving the effect of tailing away and blending into the grass or shrubs. Situations where this might be used are indicated in Figure 74.

One other material that is very useful for constructing lightweight screens is brushwood or trimmings (Figure 73). Here, cut branches complete with twigs are packed between cross pieces to create a very pleasant rustic effect that blends easily with the colours and textures of the surrounding garden. As with low hedges, the screens become part of the overall scene and divide the garden with more subtlety than the more formal bamboo screens.

Finally, hedges, whether specifically planted or created from trimmed shrub groups, can be used on boundaries or as internal dividers, but the squared-off, box-hedge effect, popular in Western gardens should be avoided since this will, like all use of symmetry, detract from the feeling of naturalness that is so important in a Japanese garden.

The choice of materials, size and style for a screen or fence will depend on a number of factors. As we have seen, one is personal taste, another is availability of the various materials, and a third is the position and precise role the unit will play. To offer some guidelines on this third factor Figure 74 shows some of the more common uses for screens and dividing fences.

The first point to notice is that the seven examples are a mixture of

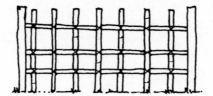

Figure 70.   Single-pole bamboo fence.

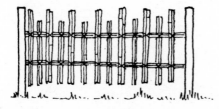

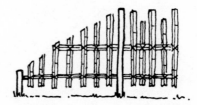

Figure 71a.   Double-pole bamboo
fence.

Figure 71b.   Double-pole bamboo
fence with sloped end.

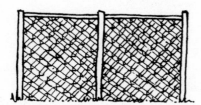

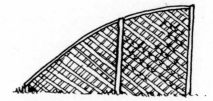

Figure 72a.   Crisscross bamboo
fencing.

Figure 72b.   Crisscross bamboo fence
with sloped end.

Figure 73.   Brushwood fencing.

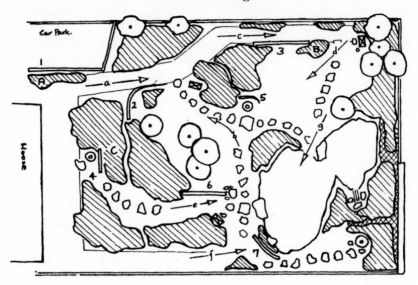

Figure 74.   Diagram illustrating the use of interior screens and fences.
   ■   solid
   ☐   see-through
1. ■ lapped-panel fence (Figure 68, approx. 6 ft high)
2. ☐ sloped-end crisscross bamboo fencing (Figure 72b approx. 3 ft–4 ft high)
3. ☐ single-pole bamboo fencing (Figure 70, approx. 4 ft high)
4. ■ solid bamboo screen (Figure 69, approx, 6 ft high)
5. ☐ sloped-end crisscross bamboo fencing (Figure 72b. approx. 4 ft high)
6. ☐ crisscross bamboo fencing (Figure 72a, approx. 3 ft–4 ft high)
7. ■ brushwood screens (Figure 73, approx. 5 ft high)

solid and see-through designs, and that they all work in combination with other features of the garden; they have specific purposes and are integrated in the overall design.

No. 1 is a solid, lapped panel fence that divides the main garden from another area (in this example a car park) not included in the Japanese design. It serves in a sense as an interior boundary being high and solid enough to completely cut off the area behind and provide the backdrop to this corner of the garden. The immediate effect of this large, regular fence can be softened by careful planting in front of it: shrub group A.

Fence no. 2 has two roles to play. Along sight line 'a.' it separates the path, and shrubs to the left of the path, from the bulk of the garden away to the right. Its purpose is not to shut off the garden but to focus attention on the path (and its decorative surface, such as that in Figure 54) and the shrubs, reserving the view of the garden until

100

the stepping-stone path is reached. It acts to define the view along sight line 'a.' and, in its second role, as a pleasant backdrop to the view from sight line 'b.'.

Fence no. 3 plays a similar role along the top section of the path, leading the eye to the lantern at the end of the path and forming a background to the view from the pond. Since this fence is of a squared-off design, the end of it should be softened and partially hidden by planting: shrub group B.

No. 4 is a bamboo screen added behind the water bowl to create an independent feature group. This has the effect of emphasizing the bowl, making it a point of interest visible from the house or terrace, and of cutting off direct sight lines into the garden. This makes the path leading away round the screen all the more inviting, since the garden behind is obscured. To avoid this screen looking too stark, however, it should be well supported by the height and bulk of shrub group C.

Screen no. 5 and fence no. 6 are both integrated features in the main part of the garden. Their role is to emphasize features and sight lines, to add to the variety of shapes in the garden, but they should not stand out too much or impose themselves on their surroundings. To ensure this does not happen, they should not be too high. No. 5, a small, compact screen sloping down into the ground, provides a background to the water bowl and an interesting shape amongst the informality of the planting. It should blend into the neighbouring shrubs and not be overconspicuous when viewed from sight line 'd.'. Fence no. 6, of lightweight bamboo, focuses sight line 'e.' on the path-dividing stone and the pond beyond it, and is integrated at one end into the shrubs and at the other into the small group of stones. From the other side, fence no. 6, in conjunction with fence no. 2, helps frame the wide area of planting and trees that makes up an important part of the garden.

No. 7 is a brushwood screen serving two specific purposes. From behind, it forms the focal point for sight line 'f.' along the path, and hides the pond until the stepping-stone path is reached. From the front, the screen forms the backdrop for the feature stone, set at the edge of the pond, and creates an alternative focal point for sight line 'g.' (the waterfall being the other).

The fences and screens in Figure 74, are meant as examples of what can be achieved by using interior dividers to accentuate certain features and create general spaces. Shrubs (as seen in Figure 49 and 53) can serve a similar purpose, but the addition of fences and screens will add variety and interest, without detracting from the informal atmosphere. As with the other components covered in this chapter, it is always worth experimenting a bit with different ideas until the desired effect is achieved.

2: GROUP RELATIONSHIPS

In the first section of this chapter we have looked in detail at the component groups needed for creating a Japanese style garden. In this second section I want to outline some of the uses to which these groups can be put: how they can be used individually, or in combination for part or all of the garden.

Before going on to these relationships, however, I should like to recap on two of the general points of design that lie behind them that we have touched on earlier in the book.

Perhaps the most important of these is the asymmetric approach to layout and the use of triangles as a guiding shape. This idea should govern not only the construction of an actual group, but also the way in which groups are juxtapositioned in the garden. This applies whatever the scale of the work and should be planned around the sight lines and focal points that make best use of the space available.

Secondly, the route by which a group is approached, or by which groups are joined, should be allowed for. This is because, as we have seen, the way in which paths are used can be vital to creating the best overall effect and realizing the full potential of a view or feature.

To help put these designs into some kind of context, I have divided them into four categories: groups for corners or screened areas of gardens, small yards and passageways, pond groups and larger-scale work. These basic ideas can then be extended or combined to suit almost any requirements.

In the first category we will look at designs for corners, screened groups in the body of the garden, or features for open-plan front gardens. Designs for these groups should concentrate on blending them around one feature or focal point and for this, combinations of rock groups and one or other of the garden ornaments provide a good basis. (In Figure 75 we can see how a water-bowl group is integrated with a rock group set as the background, and how together they provide a feature suitable for use in corners.) Secondly, because layouts in these locations cannot be viewed from many angles, the possible sight lines will be very limited. In this case the

102

best available should be chosen and the layout planned around it. Thirdly, the background should be considered. This can be either raised mounds or dense planting and will depend on the desired effect. Generally an ornament or rock group combine well with planting, shrubs and small trees, while any of the water features will require mounds.

With these things in mind we will look at a layout suitable for a corner site. In Figure 75 a water-bowl group is integrated into a rock group set as the background and together they provide a feature that acts as focal point for one main sight line. The layout illustrated in this figure, as in those that follow, is just one example of the many ways in which this combination could be used. Trying a few ideas out to find the most satisfactory is a good idea.

In Figure 75 attention focuses on the assembly of rocks and the water-bowl placed slightly in front, which has the effect of drawing the eye away from the corner. Although the actual site may be narrow, the rocks leading away from the central group help provide a sense of space while providing cohesion over the whole layout. To construct a layout like this, the rock group and its relationship to the bowl should be worked out first, to ensure that it has the right weight and balance, and the planting should then be added to provide a suitable background for it. The trees are positioned to frame the whole corner and break up the line of the fences, while the shrubs support the rocks, filling in spaces and blending the outline.

Figure 75a.   Combination of a water-bowl and rock group laid out to fill the corner of a garden.

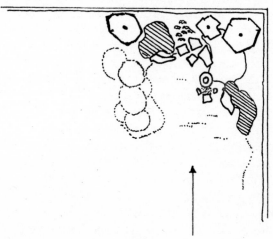

103

Figure 75b.   The rock group holds the centre of attention and leads the eye down to the bowl. Shrubs and taller trees fill out and frame the scene.

The use of a feature shrub behind the rocks helps to create the focal point, adding colour and varied shapes. Working with the trees, the larger bushes down the left-hand side both balance the mass of rocks and shrubs opposite and also screen off parts of the garden not required for this feature. The grass leading up to and in front of the group will want to be kept short to prevent it from breaking up the scene, while under the bushes it can be allowed to grow longer to add to the screening effect.

This layout would work just as well if a lantern were substituted for the rocks, or if the rock group stood on its own. A look at the actual construction of the rock and bowl groups will show that both are complete in themselves and, while in this example they are used together, either could in fact be used as a single feature. This versatility of design makes possible a large number of layouts and should be used to its fullest extent.

Used in a slightly different way these ideas can form the basis for a screened feature in the middle or along the side of a garden. The screens are used to separate the feature from other parts of the garden and form the boundaries for it. Figure 76 shows how a very interesting feature can be created, independent of whatever surrounds it. Here the overall effect has been heightened by creating a shallow depression, with the earth thus removed being built up behind it. Altering the ground level in this way helps to differentiate the feature group from its immediate surroundings, and also means that slightly smaller trees and bushes can be used in the back planting, since they will not have to be very high to screen out unwanted views.

Figure 76a.   A water bowl situated in a sunken area provides a focal point for the rocks and shrubs in this screened layout.

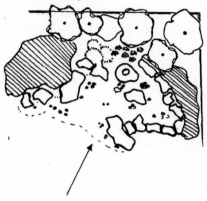

Figure 76b.   A tranquil, self-contained feature, independent of the parts of the garden that surround it.

The sunken area in this example has been used as a basis for a water-bowl and rock assembly. Around the bowl, rocks line the edge of the depression, and two larger feature rocks stand in the foreground balancing the dense planting that builds up behind the bowl. To further set the feature apart from the grass that leads away from it the floor of the enclosed area has been covered with small pebbles that give the whole layout a distinctive character. The group is designed to create an atmosphere of its own, something different and unexpected in what may otherwise be a standard garden layout. The effect of this could be heightened if water were fed into the bowl from a spout and then allowed to drip down the sides as it overflowed, adding sound and movement to the variety of textures and colours already present in the design.

This is something which would also be suggested by the next example (Figure 77) where rocks and pebbles are used in the *karesansui* style, to represent a waterfall, making an interesting and practical feature for an openplan front garden. The rocks in this layout have been arranged so that the three big central ones suggest the course of the waterfall; falling from the higher ground amongst the shrubs, around the water-dividing stone and out into a small pool. It could be part of a far larger waterfall, a place where the water gathers before falling again, or a short reach in the course of a stream. However it is interpreted, the group will create a small area of interest in the wider sweep of the garden.

When designing a feature like this, allowance should be made for the fact that the rocks will be visible from a number of different directions. This will mean that the rocks leading away from the fall should be set as low as possible, leaving the front of the arrangement open over a wide angle. In this situation the actual featured rocks or ornament, in our example, the fall, are the centre of attention, and so it is these that should be highlighted rather than the supporting parts. Equally the backplanting of shrubs will also look best if kept low and dense. This also serves to make the group more practical for a maintenance point of view, since densely planted, low shrubs need very little attention.

The position of the feature shown in Figure 77b, is, of course, only one of many possibilities. The group could occupy almost any position along the back edge of the garden, or be brought out into the centre. If this were done the back planting should be dense around the fall and lead away on either side to give the group a sense of solidity.

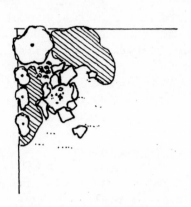

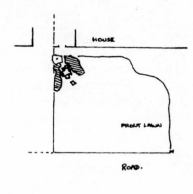

Figure 77a.   Front-garden feature in the *karesansui* style. Rocks and pebbles are used to suggest a small waterfall.

Figure 77b.   Possible position for such a feature in an open-plan garden.

Figure 77c.   The back planting breaks up the lines of the buildings and panel fence and emphasizes the arrangement of the rocks.

107

The layout examples shown in Figures 75, 76 and 77 aim to create Japanese-style features that can be used as independent units in corners or more central parts of gardens. The ideas, with suitable modifications, are interchangeable, the dry waterfall, for example, could be featured in the sunken area shown in Figure 76 instead of the water bowl, and the way they are used here are suggestions that should be seen as an indication of what can be done. The scope is very wide indeed. It is not quite so wide, however, for our next category of sites: passageways and small areas.

In these situations the space available, the shape of the space, its closed-in nature and the lack of sight lines inevitably limits the possibilities of what can be used. In Japan, though, the designers rarely miss an opportunity to create a small feature or layout, even in the awkward passages that lead from the front to the back of a house, or a space between buildings. Often, as you walk through the buildings, or along the side of one, there is something to catch and occupy the eye before you emerge into the main garden. In the two examples that follow, I have tried to indicate the scope available from a basic design to something a bit more elaborate. It should be remembered, however, that even if there is simply not enough space to construct any feature it is possible to design an interesting floor surface along the lines of the decorative paths shown in Figures 59–63.

Figure 78 is an example of a basic, easily constructed passageway feature. It, or variations on it, would be suitable for any narrow, closed-in passage where a lack of light and space makes it hard to grow plants successfully. The idea behind this sort of layout is to create a feature or area that absorbs the eye, leading it away from the textures and lines of the brick walls or concrete floor of the passageway. As can be seen in Figure 78b, it does not have to be very elaborate or involve a lot of complicated construction and could indeed consist simply of a rock group set amongst potted plants in one corner. The interest created by the arrangement shown, how-ever, comes from the combination of elements and actually uses the blank expanses of wall and floor to achieve its full effect. This principle goes back to the ideas we have looked at before where, for example, blank spaces were an integral part of the old Chinese scroll paintings and the *karesansui* garden designs later developed in Japan.

Depending on the size of the site, the rocks and pebbles should be kept in some kind of scale. If the site allows the use of a few large, bulky rocks then these should be surrounded by larger, regular-sized

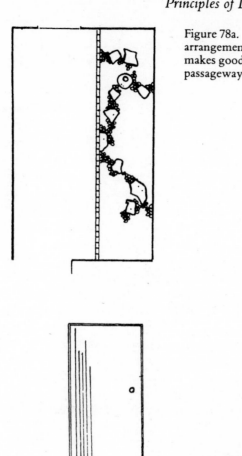

Figure 78a.   A stone-and-pebble arrangement, featuring a water bowl, makes good use of an awkward passageway site.

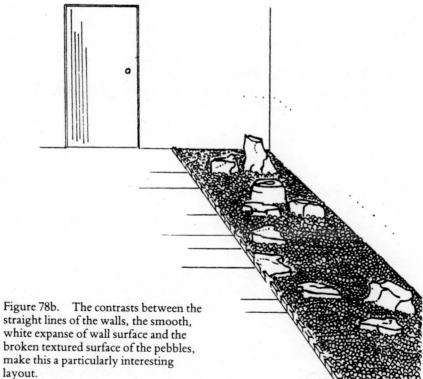

Figure 78b.   The contrasts between the straight lines of the walls, the smooth, white expanse of wall surface and the broken textured surface of the pebbles, make this a particularly interesting layout.

pebbles. If smaller rocks are used they should be positioned amongst small pebbles or gravel. The guiding point here is that the different components of the layout should be in scale with each other to give an overall coherence to the group.

If this is done successfully, the scale of the layout relative to what surrounds it will take care of itself. Once constructed, the design shown in Figure 78b will need no further attention except a regular spraying with water. Wetting the stones and pebbles keeps their colours bright and fresh and makes them more interesting to look at.

Passing now from the passageway into the small yard site we have a more intricate layout that combines rocks, shrubs and a screen. The site illustrated in Figure 79 contains a number of requirements that must be taken into consideration when planning the layout, which are typical of the kind of thing that must be allowed for in a yard of this nature, and we will look at them quickly before going on to the design. First, there must be good access, in this case from the gate to the door and round the side of the house. Second, there must be somewhere for the bins and a coal bunker that is convenient to the house and that does not intrude on the garden design. Thirdly, some space is usually required for storage or parking bicycles and, again, this should be separated as much as possible from the planted area. Thus the yard must be divided into practical and decorative areas as equally as circumstances allow.

As can be seen in Figure 79a the yard is split into three distinct parts. One, behind the screen, for the amenities, a second on the left of the path for practical uses, and a third to the right where the plants, rocks and lantern bring some colour and interest to the whole area. The illusion of space for the first is created by building out a wide step in front of the door and taking the path from there. The screen runs from opposite this point back to the wall making a neat, hidden area for the bunker, or shed, and the dustbins.

The yard then runs down the length of the path as a single area and the space behind the screen does not intrude on the arrangement in front of it. The path itself then divides the rest of the yard into two and the layout of rocks and plants can be tailored to the amount of space left. Although the layout for the yard can be more elaborate than that for the passageway, it should not contain too much, either rocks, ornaments or combinations of these, since it can very easily look too crowded and thus contrived. Given the dimensions of the space available, decide on the main feature, in this example a lantern, and build around it using a minimum of components: a rock or two,

Figure 79a.   Allowance has been made in this design for the practical uses of the small yard.

Figure 79b.   A light screen, the boundary wall and a decorative path frame the layout of rocks and a small lantern, and separate it from the other parts of the yard.

some low shrubs and one or two taller bushes or trees. Understatement is the key to good results.

From concentrating on the smaller areas of gardens, the corners passageways and yards, I will look now at the details of layout for the third and fourth categories, ponds and other larger work. A number of designs that fall into these categories have already been discussed in detail in the first section of this chapter (see Figures 31, 32, 47, 49, 53, 74). These, taken with the examples we will look at now, demonstrate the wide scope possible by the versatility of Japanese design.

Ponds, as I have already mentioned, form a very important part of Japanese gardens and in the next two examples I would like to give an indication of the potential of this medium. (These layouts, and others earlier in the book, can of course contain water or be dry in the *karesansui* style.) The plan in Figure 80 is based around a small pond that features a particularly interesting waterfall, while Figure 81 illustrates how a pair of small waterfalls can form the nucleus for a combination of rocks and water.

In Figure 80 the components combine to focus the attention on the waterfall. The way the feature rocks around the pond have been laid, and the positioning of the two island stones both draw the eye towards the elegant, single fall which emerges from the built-up stone group and drops into the pond below. Additional emphasis is provided by the two featured plants, a small tree jutting out over the fall and a large shrub on the other side. Although the fall and pond

Figure 80a.   A pond layout designed around a featured waterfall.

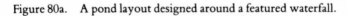
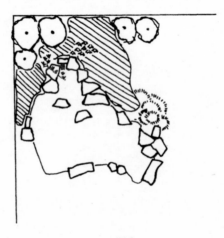

Figure 80b.   The rocks and plants concentrate attention on the high, narrow waterfall.

may not be very big, the back planting has been used to suggest distance, with large shrub groups behind and smaller shrubs coming down around the pool. This type of layout is particularly suitable for sites with distinct level changes since these can be used to build higher waterfalls than would be practical on a flatter site. (Figures 81 and 82 illustrate how level sites can be made more interesting by creating slight level changes.)

The success of a layout like the one shown in Figure 80 lies in creating or suggesting sufficient detail to make it interesting without overcrowding the area, which will obscure the focal point and distract the eye. Once the rocks forming the required bulk for the fall have been assembled, other details such as the islands and the feature stones round the pool should be positioned to balance and support the fall group, until the whole layout has the right proportions. Once this is achieved, nothing else should be added, since an extra island or large feature stone might start to clutter up the design, and thus destroy its overall cohesion.

The same points will also apply to the construction of the layout shown in Figure 81 although here, rather than concentrating on one focal point, we have in effect a series of smaller individual points of interest which blend into a larger scheme when looked at together. This layout would be suitable for either a gently sloping site or a level site that can be built up towards the back with soil taken from the pool areas. In either case, three levels are required. One, the highest, for the rock group and waterfall at the top end of the upper pond, one for the upper pond itself, and a third for the lower pond. Since neither of the falls need be particularly high this is quite easy to arrange when digging out. (This will not be sufficient however, for the layout in Figure 80, since the height of the fall would need a lot of building up from level.)

The main difference in design and approach between this layout and that in Figure 80 is that here each section, the two pools, their waterfalls, feature stones and back planting, can be designed as a separate unit and become a focal point in their own right. This works as an overall design because their basic similarities will help blend them into one overall scheme when viewed from a slight distance. This does not apply to Figure 80 where one element, the pool, serves to highlight the other, the waterfall, and should not be designed separately.

Another point to be noticed about this layout can be seen in Figure 81b. Unlike a number of previous designs where the correct atmosphere for the focal point has been created by high, dense planting that suggests, for example, streams in mountain gorges and where the imagination is stimulated by the suggestion of seclusion

Figure 81a.   Gently sloping ground is used here to create a series of ponds and waterfalls leading away from a corner of a garden.

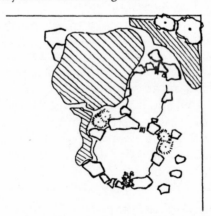

Figure 81b.   Large feature rocks, rather than planting, are used to frame the scene, emphasizing the wide sweep of the design.

and solitariness, here the design is much more open and spread over a wider area. In this case the layout is framed by large but rather flat rocks that extend the contours of the pool-side rocks, rather than by tall trees and large shrubs which in this context might tend to overshadow the pool layout. This also, incidentally, makes it easier to use the pools as the feature part of the garden, since they will not be isolated behind tall banks of shrubs and can easily be integrated with their immediate surroundings.

Finally, we come on to a layout that introduces Japanese design to a large part of the garden, combining a number of components that we have looked at, bringing them together over an extended area. The three main components on which it centres are the water-bowl group, approached by the stepping-stone path, the pool with its single-span bridge, and the rock group set out of sight amongst the shrubs at the back (Figure 82).

115

To create this layout, soil taken from the pool has been built up behind it to form the background for itself and the water-bowl group. At the same time the higher ground surrounds and obscures the lower area in the corner which becomes an ideal setting for a small, secluded rock group.

In Figure 82 the techniques used to combine the different components into larger layouts can be identified. The rocks and planting used for the pool and, in this case, the bridge, give us a basic scale to work from. This governs the size and amount of planting that leads away to other areas, which in turn are designed to fit in with it. In this way the rock group, although out of sight from the front, will be constructed to suit the space available and size of shrubs around it. Similarly, the bowl and its supporting stones will blend in with the higher ground behind and the size of stone used along the pool side. On another level, a stepping stone path is used for the approach to the whole layout since this best suits the informality of the overall design and will not distract attention from it by its own appearance. Finally, the planting is designed to fill out the background rather than highlight individual focal points (which is how it is used in Figure 80), and for this reason does not feature any particularly outstanding shrub or tree. Created to be approached and walked

Figure 82.   A layout for larger work that features a number of interesting focal points. Soil from the elongated pool is built up within the dotted lines to create a basis for the whole design.

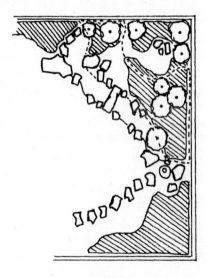

Figure 83.   Seen from the stepping-stone path, the pool takes on the appearance of a stream, while the bridge leads the eye up the path behind to an, as yet, hidden view.

amongst, this layout offers a variety of views depending on where the viewer is standing, rather than one integrated view to be looked at from a distance.

As we have seen in this section on group relationships, layouts should be planned around the natural assets of the site, not only to blend better with the overall character of the garden, but also to avoid excessive work. If the garden slopes steeply then it may be best exploited by the kind of design shown in Figure 80. If it is generally level then the ideas in Figures 81 and 82 may be more suitable. The layout chosen will also, of course, depend to some extent on time, money and materials available, but it should be kept in mind that one of the essential ingredients of successful design in a Japanese style is that the result should look as natural as possible, as though it could always have been there, and to do this the initial idea of the layout should be developed from the nature of the site itself and its surroundings.

4

Construction Work

In this chapter we will be looking at the detailed construction work needed to create the groups and layouts that we have covered in earlier parts of the book, but first some more general points need discussion. When making a garden, whether or not it is done in a Japanese style, there are four distinct stages of the operation. First there must be a period of deciding what to have, then comes the planning, or deciding where to put what, third the construction work, and finally the planting of trees, shrubs and flowers. If each of these stages is given equal attention then the garden is likely to be a success; if not, at some point or other, problems will arise, at best holding up work, and at worst spoiling the look of the finished project or making it unsuitable for the uses to which it is going to be put. Planning and design work is considered crucial to success in Japan, where even today construction teams work not only from plans, but also from detailed artist's impressions of a finished group or layout, used on site to ensure that the work is as accurate as possible. Time spent on this planning phase of construction is considered well used, since what might take you a day to put up will be looked at for many years hence.

During the decision stage of the work two main points should be considered. The first is: who will use the garden and what will they use it for? When this is clear, the garden can be designed to suit these needs and the part or parts that will be in Japanese style can be concentrated on. This brings us on to the second point: what type of Japanese design suits the particular garden best? Thought should be given here to the amount of work that can be done, the suitability of a pond, or a working waterfall. Can the necessary rocks and components be acquired, or should the garden be in *karesansui* style? Is there a view worth including in the *shakkei* style, and can the right

118

atmosphere for a particular kind of group be created? The point behind this deliberation is that while the plants and trees are relatively easy to alter later, it is not so simple to change a layout or feature, and once a feature is constructed it will not be satisfactory if the back planting cannot be completed for reasons such as space or inconvenience to neighbours.

Once these decisions have been taken it is time to move on to planning, and this includes not only the new feature or layout but taking existing garden characteristics into consideration as well. Plan the layout around the garden and your other requirements. This means using the slopes and shapes of the garden allowing for the various access routes necessary (either for cars, or reaching sheds or vegetable plots), existing features such as manholes or clothes lines and sight lines for good views outside the garden, as the basis for the new design. In addition to these considerations, if you are likely to do more work in the future, such as extending a layout, make sure that the group or feature you construct first can whenever required be joined to the new work, so that it does not at a later date look isolated and out of place.

With the decisions and detailed planning out of the way, we pass on to the third stage, the construction work.

If the garden, or part of the garden, to be worked on is not above average size then the work described here can generally be done by one person, who will probably only need help when it comes to moving big stones or laying concrete. When doing such jobs, particularly concreting, be sure to have an assistant ready or you may end up wasting both time and costly materials. The tools required you will probably already have, or can easily borrow, and more specialized items such as cement mixers can be hired by the day at reasonable rates from most tool-hire companies. The methods of construction described here and the materials used are intended to give a general knowledge of what can be done and most can be adapted and used in various ways, with a variety of finishes, provided the basic principles are followed carefully throughout.

1. Ponds and waterfalls

Ponds
The size, depth and position of the pond must be decided on during the planning stage, and so too should the question as to whether or not the earth dug from the pond area is required for building up

119

backing mounds or whether it is to be removed from the site altogether. This depends on how large the pond will be, but if there is going to be any excess soil, a refuse skip should be hired to take it away. If the pond is going to feature a large waterfall, prepare the site for this at the same time as the pond to ensure that the positioning and height of the waterfall rocks will produce the desired effect. Generally speaking, however, before starting work the size and positioning of any backing mounds, allowing for the amount of slope of the existing site, should be carefully worked out so that as the pond is dug, material taken from it can either be built up to create the new layout, lost on other parts of the garden, or put straight into the skip for removal. This planning can save an enormous amount of time and effort.

The amount of soil that must be removed from the pond area will depend to a certain extent on the type of material to be used on the bottom, the thickness of the edges (rocks along the edge require more space than, for example, a pebble beach), and whether or not there is to be a double-span bridge and islands. I will look at these various alternatives in a moment, but first I would like to outline the general technique for pond construction that ensures that a man-made pond looks as natural as possible. Figure 84 illustrates all the important aspects of construction. Before looking at it in detail, I would like to reiterate some general points. For successful natural-looking results none of the materials of which the pond is constructed should be visible above the surface. In the example shown here it is important that the concrete skin on the bottom does not show at the edges but is well coverd by the edging material. Second, it is a good idea to avoid piled-up stones at the edges or as islands, since these inevitably have a contrived effect. Thus the design and depth of the pond should ensure that single rocks can be used along the edge or as islands, so that there are clean, uncluttered shapes reaching down to the bottom (see Figure 34). Finally, it is essential that you have a clear idea of where the water level will come so that the edges and islands can be set at the right depth. If you want to build a small pool overshadowed by rocks, in the style of a mountain stream (see Figure 80) then the rocks at the edges will want to stand high above the water, and for more open styles of pool, such as that shown in Figure 81, the rocks will need to sit well down in the water. This is worth giving some thought to since it will be very hard to alter at a later date.

Concentrating on the general technique first, Figure 84b illustrates

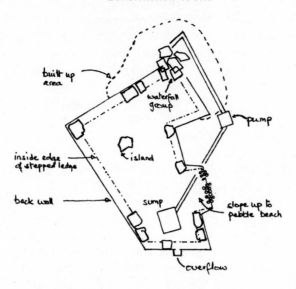

Figure 84a.   Construction plan for a pond, illustrating details for a waterfall, pebble beach, pump, sump and overflow.

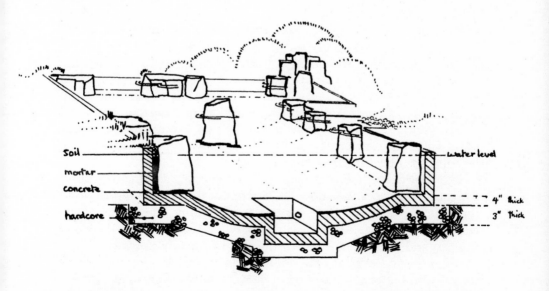

Figure 84b.   Section of the pond showing details that are out of sight once the pond is completed.

121

how the pond is blended into the area around it. First the shape is dug out, and for large concrete-skinned ponds, all loose, vegetable soil must be removed, down to the firm subsoil. Once this is reached, a layer of hard core 3 in (8 cm) thick is laid and compacted. The most suitable material for this, and any other jobs requiring a firm base, such as paths, is obtainable from quarries and should consist of small stones of approximately 1 in (2.5 cm) diameter. On top of the hard core comes a 4 in (10 cm) layer of concrete (mixed at a strength of 1 part cement to 6 parts sand and gravel, i.e. 1:6) laid across the bottom and up the sides of the pond forming a stepped ledge along the edge. The edging material, in this case rocks, are then laid along the sides fixed firmly to the concrete on a bed of mortar. (Mortar is a combination of building sand and cement, mixed for most purposes in a ratio of 1 part cement to 4 parts sand, i.e. 1:4.) The mortar is brought up behind the rock until water level is reached and then soil is used to fill up behind and between the rocks until ground level is reached. In this way the concrete sides of the pond and mortar joints between the rocks are all out of sight below ground and water level. When positioning the stones on the stepped ledge, bring them forward until there is a slight overhang. This creates dark shadows around the base of the stones when the pond is filled and adds interest and realism to the finished effect.

In cases where a waterfall is to be fed from the pond itself, a pump will need to be installed to take water from the sump, set at the lowest point of the pond, and deliver it to the top of the fall. A variety of pumps are available – consult a dealer as to which is the most suitable for your needs. Place the pump in an underground chamber to remove it from sight and eliminate any sound. The sump in fact serves a number of purposes and the pond bottom should be sloped gently down to it from all sides. This means that when the pond is drained for cleaning or repairs, fish and unwanted matter will be collected here for easy removal.

The next details for consideration are the beach and the overflow. In Figure 85a we can see how the bottom of the pond is sloped up to the beach area, rather than stepped as it is along other parts of the edges. The pebbles are then laid across the join between the pond bottom and the soil, and down the slope to below the water level, giving a natural effect to the whole feature. An overflow should be included in the plan for any pond that contains a substantial amount of water, and particularly those that are fed by an existing stream. Situated at surface level the overflow will not only drain off excess

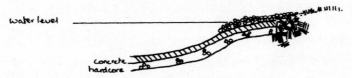

Figure 85a.   Bottom of the pond sloped up to create an area for a pebble beach (section).

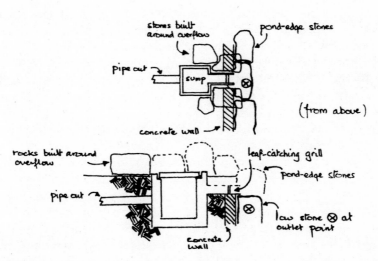

Figure 85b.   Design for pond overflow (section).

water, but also, because of the steady, gentle flow through it, act as a collecting place for dead leaves or other material floating on the pond's surface. A good, basic design for this purpose is shown in Figure 85b. Here, leaves and sticks are caught in the grill, while smaller debris collects in the sump. The whole arrangement is set just below ground level and covered by rocks so as to be hardly noticeable.

As is clear from the above, concrete is one material suitable for the pond bottom. The other material that can be used is plastic sheeting which is laid and hidden from view along the same lines as concrete. The advantages and disadvantages of the two materials are fairly obvious. Concrete is by far the more durable and once laid provides a solid foundation on which a variety of features can be built. Basically, unless building a small pool, it is better to use concrete for its strength and long life, although a plastic sheet is much quicker and easier to use since it does not require so much preparation or technique to lay it.

With plastic sheeting, planning and digging out is the same as detailed above. The sheet can be either black or clear plastic and should be of the thick type used for damp courses in buildings. Rolls can be easily bought at most builders merchants. To lay it, compact the subsoil in the bottom of the pond and cover it evenly with a 1 in (2.5 cm) thick layer of building sand. Spread the sheet out over this, covering the bottom and running up the sides as far as the concrete shown in Figure 84b. The rocks for the edges are then carefully positioned on it, sitting on a bed of mortar, the sheet pulled up tight behind them and secured in place by mortar pushed down between it and the rock. All other details are the same as for concrete bottoms. If the pond is too large to be covered by a single sheet it is probably wiser to use concrete.

To concrete the pond, work should be divided into two parts. First the bottom and the stepped ledge should be covered with fairly dry concrete that can be smoothed down with the back of a shovel. Allow this to set for a minimum of two days and then erect shuttering for the sides on the ledge. Shuttering means the wooden boards set up to hold the concrete while it goes off. Once it is set, remove the shutters. Figure 86 illustrates how the shutters should be arranged for pond walls. The most suitable material for these shutters would be boards of 1 in (2.5 cm) plywood cut to the right height and laid 4 in (10 cm) apart along the step. They should then be held firmly in place along the top and bottom by small pieces of wood nailed across the gap. (When you remove the shuttering leave the bottom crosspieces in place under the wall.) The whole structure must then be held firmly in place by props at the front, and earth filled in behind. Now pour your concrete into the shutters, ram it firmly down and allow it to set for one, two or three days, before removing the shutters. Finally, when all the shuttering and props have been taken out, the rocks and features for the pond can be added. If a sump is being included in the pond, the floor of the sump should be laid first and the sides added with shuttering when this is set. The top edges are then covered when the bottom of the pond is laid.

For an average-sized pond set in well-drained ground, an approved water proofer added to the concrete as it is being mixed should prevent any leakage. If, however, you need a totally water-tight pond two techniques can be used. One is to lay a plastic sheet

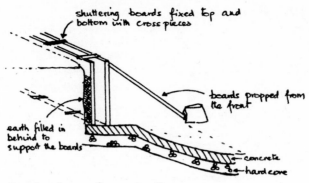

Figure 86.   Erecting shutters for pond walls.

on top of the hard core and lay the concrete on top; the other is to paint the concrete's surface with a bituminous waterproofer. Then cover the waterproofer with an additional layer of mortar about 2 in (5 cm) thick, (mix the mortar 1:4) to protect the surface.

To position single-stone islands, choose a suitable rock and then mortar it firmly to the pond bottom, as shown in figure 84b. To construct a larger, built-up island which can be planted, follow the procedure in Figure 87. Here a ring of stones are mortared together and all gaps between them sealed with small stones and mortar. The space inside is then filled up to water level with a combination of small rocks and hard core and the surface covered with soil. Any feature stones or plants required can now be arranged on top.

One last detail of construction needs mentioning before we pass on to waterfalls. If the pond is to feature a double-span bridge that will need a support stone in the middle, the stepped ledge round the pond should be continued across the pond at the bridging point to ensure a good foundation for the spans and eliminate the need to build up a number of stones for the support. This is illustrated in Figure 88 and, if used, should be constructed at the same time as the rest of the pond bottom.

Waterfalls

When deliberating about what kind of waterfall to construct, use the various types shown in the first part of Chapter 3 as a starting point. Whether you want a combination falls, such as in Figure 24, a single featured fall, as in Figure 80, or a series of falls like those shown in Figure 81, the basic shapes should be built up from the examples in Figures 17–22. These ideas can then be elaborated on and developed

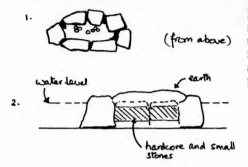

1.

(from above)

water level   earth

2.

hardcore and small stones

(cut-away section)

Figure 87.   Building up an island for planting. Rocks mortared together on pond bottom (1); filled first with hard core and small stones, and then covered with earth for planting (2).

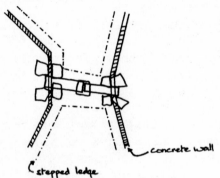

concrete wall

stepped ledge

Figure 88.   Supporting a double-span bridge. To ensure firm foundations for a double-span bridge, the stepped ledge along the sides of the pond is continued across the bridging point in a raised bridge. The support stone and bridge spans are then placed across it.

until the fall is as you want it. Once the type of flow (i.e. left-hand, right-hand, double and so on) has been chosen, the rest of the fall should be designed to fit the particular layout in question. Before completing the design, however, you should be sure that you have, or can get, suitable stones, because these will determine as much as anything what the finished fall will look like.

Once the stone has been obtained, build a mock-up of the finalized layout so that you are sure that you have the right stone shapes to fit your design. Once you are certain about this, building can begin. The next problem is to obtain the correct flow down the fall once the water is turned on. This depends partly on the surfaces of the stones and partly on the rate of flow. The stones forming the actual path of the fall should therefore be chosen for their surface textures as well as their shape (see Chapter 3, p. 61), so that you build into the fall certain flow characteristics which can then be regulated by the rate at which the water is allowed to pass down the fall.

This is a matter of experimentation once the water is turned on and regulated by opening up or closing down the stop tap. For low falls between ponds, for example, this cannot be so carefully controlled and in these cases the stone over which the water passes is the deciding factor. It will be clear from the above that stone selection is an all-important part of building falls and is worth spending some time on.

Now for assembling and constructing the fall. For a detailed description of how a large fall group is assembled please see Appendix 1, which contains a step-by-step account of the construction of a waterfall in the garden of an old people's home in Osaka, Japan. It illustrates, I hope, not only the construction details, but also the meticulous care with which even contemporary Japanese landscape gardeners approach this work. For now, however, we will look at basic technique.

Figures 89a, b, and c illustrate the successive stages in construction, which is not in itself particularly complicated. First the pond edge stone is positioned against the wall and mortared into place. This stone should if possible be the same height as the wall, so that the second stone, which will cover the wall, can be placed on top (Figure 89a). Behind this, soil should be built up to hold the next tier of stones in place (Figure 89b), and provide a solid foundation for the whole group. Finally, stones should be added on either side to give the waterfall the desired shape and balance (Figure 89c). The overall shape and in particular the actual path of the fall can now be rounded out by the addition of smaller stones whenever needed (for fuller details see Appendix 1).

During construction of the waterfall there are two other details that will need attention. One is the water source at the top of the fall; the other is creating suitable places for small plants to be added later. If the fall is to have running water, whether the source is the mains or water pumped up from the pond, a length of 4 in (10 cm) plastic pipe should be run up the back of the group and built in during construction. The lower end of this should come just below ground level at the back, and the top just behind the highest point of the fall (see Figure 90a). Then, after construction is complete, the water pipe can be run up through this and mortared into position at the top. At some point near the base of the mound a stop tap should be fitted and built into a small chamber below ground level. Finally, at the top of the fall, at the point where the pipe emerges, a small header pool should be built to ensure that a good volume of water starts down the fall. Figure 90b illustrates how careful mortaring of the top stones

a.

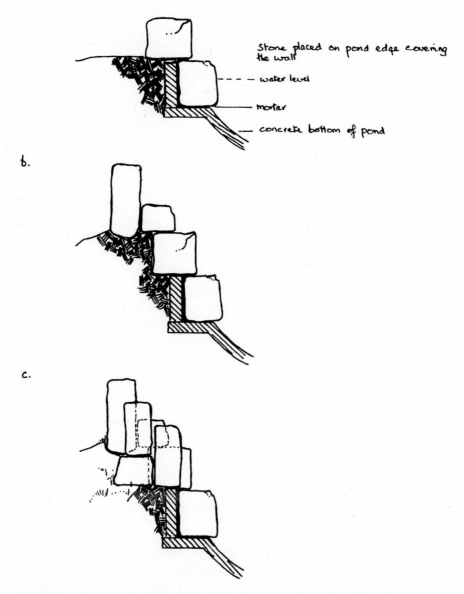

Stone placed on pond edge covering the wall

water level

mortar

concrete bottom of pond

b.

c.

Figure 89.   Construction procedure for building up a waterfall group. a. Stone placed on pond edge covering the wall. b. Soil is built up behind the stones to bring the fall up to required height. c. Stones are positioned down the sides of the soil mound to fill out the gaps.

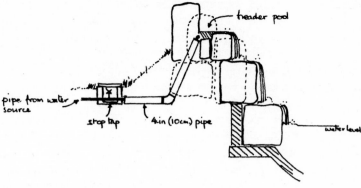

Figure 90a. Bringing water to the top of the waterfall.

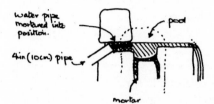

Figure 90b. Details of the header pool.

will create such a pool. For the plants, small basins (like that for the header pool) should be built at intervals down the sides of the fall path. These should be then filled with small pebbles and soil ready for planting. Useful plants for such places include ornamental grasses and ferns.

2. Water substitutes

Most of the layouts and designs that include a pond and waterfall that we have looked at have been approached on the assumption that water will be used (see, for example, Figures 80–82). There are a number of reasons, however, why the designer may choose to build them in the *karesansui*, or dry style, and in this section we will look at how to handle the two main materials that can substitute for water. As illustrated in Figures 42 and 43, the two most common substitutes are grass, kept very short, and gravel, often raked in patterns suggesting water. Whichever of these is used the preparation of the site will be similar.

When the layout for the pond has been finalized it should be marked out and then dug to a uniform depth of about 1 foot (30 cm),

129

with an additional few inches taken out round the edges where the edging stones will sit. This ensures that the stones sit firmly, with their bases out of sight (see Figure 91a). The most suitable type of gravel is 'pea gravel', laid about 1½ in (4 cm) thick. Before laying this, position the edging rocks and any islands. Then roll the pond bottom flat and cover it with a thin layer of scalping dust (available like pea gravel from most quarries). This helps seal the surface and fill in any slight hollows left after rolling. Then lay the gravel on the scalpings and rake it out evenly until the surface looks right (Figure 91b). This can then be worked into designs (as shown in Figure 43) that suggest the ripples and eddies of water in moving water. Carefully done, this can be surprisingly effective. For grass finishes the preparation is similar except that instead of covering the area in scalpings the ground should be worked as it would for laying a lawn, including digging and rolling, and then sown. Once the grass begins to grow keep it cut as short as possible and regularly weeded, since long grass stems or groups of weeds will immediately destroy the illusion we are trying to create. If you wish to encourage the growth of moss in the grass dig peat into the earth before sowing.

The *karesansui* style of garden needs to be viewed in an imaginative frame of mind but it can be helped considerably by careful attention to detail and regular maintenance.

3. Paths

Techniques for laying paths can be divided into four different types. One, the solid-bed technique, most suitable for paths with a mixture of materials of unequal thickness (crazy paving and pebbles, for

Figure 91a. Preparation of pond area for gravel or grass finish.

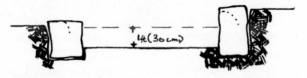

Figure 91b. Laying a gravel finish.

example). Two, mortar spots, the most practical way to lay paths of uniformly thick materials such as slabs or bricks. Three, the method for making stepping-stones paths; and four, that for laying gravel paths which need some kind of edging to prevent the gravel spreading onto beds and lawns.

The solid bed technique is illustrated in Figure 92a. To ensure a good, solid foundation, dig the path area down to firm subsoil. (If this means the level is then too deep it should be filled in with hard core until the correct depth is reached.) Assuming that the finished level of the path is to be the same as the ground level around it, the excavation depth should allow for 2 in (5 cm) of scalpings, 2 in (5 cm) of mortar bed and the overall thickness of the surface material. The subsoil is then covered with a 2 in (5 cm) layer of scalpings (if preferred, sand will do the same job), and on top of this lay the 2 in (5 cm) solid bed. (A lean mortar mix of about 1:8.) Finally, while the mortar is still wet and working in short runs, position the crazy paving and pebbles in the required patterns and push them down to a uniform finish. Ideally this should be slightly sloped to one side to ensure that rain water runs off and does not collect in puddles.

For mortar spots, preparation is the same up to and including laying the scalpings. When this has been done, blobs of a 1:4 mortar mix about 2 in (5 cm) high are positioned to receive the slabs, slates, bricks or whatever is being used (see Figure 92b). Then push the slab firmly down reducing the blobs to approximately 1 in (2.5 cm) thickness, spreading them out and making a firm bond. For paths combining for example slabs and pebbles, a combination of solid bed and mortar spot is most suitable. Lay the slabs first and then fill in the gaps with a solid bed to take the pebbles (Figure 92c).

Stepping-stone paths are by far the easiest to lay. The main considerations are spacing, levelness, firmness and positioning in relation to ground level. The procedure is as follows. Choosing flat stones, lay them out along the line of the path and check the spacing by walking along them. Adjust the gaps until you can comfortably step from one to the next. When you are satisfied with the spacing, mark the position of each stone and dig out a shallow hole for each one to sit in. Placing the stones in position one after the other, check that each is relatively level and that it is firmly held in position by packing soil in underneath and around it to eliminate any movement. The height of the stones above ground level is a matter of personal taste but as a general rule they should be as low as possible, both for ease of walking and for blending with the area around.

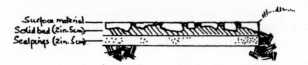

Figure 92a.   Solid–bed technique for combinations of path materials of unequal thickness.

Figure 92b.   Mortar–spot technique for path materials of uniform thickness.

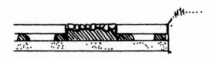

Figure 92c.   Combination of solid–bed and mortar–spot techniques.

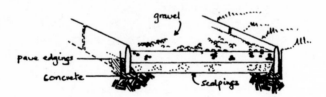

Figure 92d.   Technique for laying a gravel path with edgings.

Gravel paths are laid in the same way as gravel surfaces for *karesansui* ponds (see Figure 91b), with the addition of some kind of edging material to prevent the gravel from spreading. Old bricks laid on edge or on end look good with gravel, but concrete pave edgings are more durable and are easier to lay. (These come in standard sizes of 6 or 7 in × 3 ft × 2 in [15 or 18 cm × 90 cm × 5 cm] and are available from garden centres and builders merchants.) They are set in a small amount of concrete down the sides of the path and following its levels. When installed (see Figure 92d) the gravel is raked smooth between them.

4. Rocks and ornament groups

The most important factor in setting rocks, whether as part of a group, an individual feature, as bridge-supporting stones, a complement to an ornament, or as, we have seen, stepping stones, is that they should sit firmly in position and look as natural as possible. To be firm they must be set in a suitable hole and held tightly by soil rammed down around them. Unless you are planning to erect some particularly large stone as a feature, concrete will not be necessary. To make a stone look natural, two points should be observed: one is that a stone should sit in the ground, rather than on it, and the second is that as far as possible the stone should be positioned to match its overall shape and stratification lines. In other words a ledged rock with distinct lines would look unnatural if stood upright with the ledges and lines running vertically. Try the stone in various positions until you have decided which looks the most natural. When this is done, dig a shallow hole to hold and set the rock firmly in place.

Arranging rocks around an ornament should follow the same principles as above, with the difference that for a bowl group (either *chōzubachi* or *tsukubai*) allowance must be made for the overflow area (see Figure 50). For this dig a shallow hole and then fill it with regular hard core and a covering of decorative stones over the top. The other large stones should then be set round the rim of this to complete the group.

5. Walls, fences and screens

Walls, whatever material is used to build them, need a footing of some kind, i.e. a shallow, levelled trench which provides something firm for the wall to stand on. Depending on the type of wall, it can be either firm subsoil or concrete. Any wall that requires mortaring together (i.e. bricks, blocks or stone walls over 4 ft [120 cm]) will require a concrete footing; for dry-stone walls (built without mortar) firm earth footings will suffice.

Stone walls with earth footings

Mark out the line of the wall and clear away the grass and topsoil to a width of one foot either side of the proposed wall (see Figure 93a). Next, dig out a trench until firm subsoil is reached and level out the bottom along its length. Following this, arrange the stones in piles along the edge of the footing, making sure that each pile has its fair

133

share of small and large, good and bad stones. To build the wall, take the largest stone from each pile and place it firmly on the footing 1 ft (30 cm) from one edge of the trench, eyeing up from one end to ensure they are sitting in a straight line. Repeat this on the other side of the footing (see Figure 93b). Next, working up both sides of the wall, and filling in between them with well-compacted soil, build around and on these stones in a pyramid shape, until the pyramids meet (Figure 93c). Then, placing the largest remaining stones at the lowest points, repeat the process until the required height is reached, (Figure 93d). Finally, level off along the top of the wall (Figure 93e). (If the wall is to be higher than 4 ft [120 cm], use mortar and build on a concrete footing. See below.)

Figure 93.   Stone walls with eartn footings.

edge of trench
edge of wall   ——— ——— ——— } 1ft (30 cm)

edge of wall
edge of trench ——— ——— ——— } 1ft (30cm)

a. Marking and digging out trench for an earth footing (seen from above).

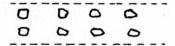

b. Placing the largest stones along the two faces of the wall (see from above).

c. Building up with smaller stones in pyramid shapes (seen from the side).

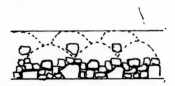

d. Repeating the process until the required height is reached (seen from the side).

e. Levelling off with small stones along the top of the wall (seen from the side).

Mortared walls with concrete footings

For concrete footings dig a trench large enough to take the concrete laid 6 in (15 cm) deep and 2 ft (60 cm) wide. The bottom of the trench should be subsoil or if this is excessively deep, made up with hard core once the subsoil is reached. When the trench is prepared, bang in a series of wooden pegs at regular intervals along it so that the peg tops are 6 in (15 cm) from the trench bottom. Using a board and spirit level, check that the pegs are level and that there is a 6 in (15 cm) clearance between the board and subsoil along the length of the footing. Make any necessary alterations now. Mix the concrete (1:6) and fill in the trench up to the peg tops, levelling off between them with your shovel. The concrete should now be left to set for at least two days.

To build a wall with concrete blocks or bricks (or any similar material of regular sizes), the easiest and most practical pattern is probably the stretcher bond (see Figure 94). To do this, first build up the two ends, or corners if there is a change of direction, and then working up course by course fill in between them, using a building line as a guide for position and levelness. Once the wall is complete, carefully point the faces by running a trowel along the mortar and down the vertical joins, filling in any holes and giving it all a uniform, smooth finish. Otherwise the finished wall will look very untidy.

Semidry stone walls are built in the same way as dry ones (see Figure 93a–b), with the exception that small stones and mortar are used to fill in between the faces instead of earth (see Figure 95). Using this technique, there will be no mortar showing on the outside giving the effect of a dry stone wall and the strength of a mortared one.

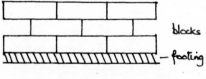

Figure 94. Standard stretcher bond for block or brick walls.

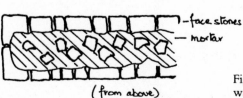

(from above)

Figure 95. Section of semi-dry stone wall showing mortar and stone filling.

A number of different fence designs can be adapted from those shown for screens in Figures 68–73, but perhaps the two most useful for long stretches around gardens are lapped panels and wire. The panel fences are used at points where something is to be blocked out or more privacy is required; the wire fences, often in combination with hedges, where more open fencing is suitable – at places, for example, that overlook a good view.

Lapped panel fences

Lapped panels come in standard sizes (3 ft to 6 ft [90 cm to 1.8 m] high by 6 ft [1.8 m] long) and are available complete with posts from most garden centres. To erect them first clear the ground along the line of the fence, removing plants and shrubs and levelling any large bumps. When the ground is clear, dig the first post hole (allowing for a minimum of 2 ft [60 cm] of post in the ground) and stand the post in it. Alter the post height until it suits the size of panel and firmly concrete it in place. Following this, dig the hole for the second post. Check the position of this by running a building line out along the line of the fence and fixing it firmly to the first post at one end and a temporary stake at the other. Nail a panel to the first post, and check that it is lying level and upright. Drop the second post into its hole, nail it to the panel and concrete it in position (see Figure 96). Continue in this way along the length of the fence, digging the post holes, fixing a panel and adding the next post until the fence is complete. When all the posts and panels are in position, go back along the fence, checking that the panels are level and the posts upright and prop them firmly in position. The props can be removed after a couple of days when the concrete has set. If the panel fence is

Figure 96.   Erection of lapped panels.

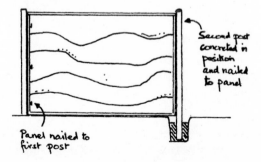

Second post concreted in position and nailed to panel

Panel nailed to first post

intended to support climbing plants, slotted concrete posts should be used, which will make the fence much stronger. First set the posts in position, using a building line and concrete, and then slide the panels down into position when the posts have set firm.

Wire fences

To be strong enough to keep a good tension on the wire, these fences need two kinds of post, strainers and prick posts. The strainers – at either end, every 25 yds (23 m) along the length, and at any changes of direction – will need to be 4 in × 4 in × 5 ft or 6 ft (10 cm × 10 cm × 1.5 m or 1.8 m) treated softwood with props of similar proportions. End strainers need one prop and middle strainers two (see Figure 97). Between the strainers, at a rate of one per yard you will need softwood prick posts (4 ft or 5 ft [1.2 or 1.5 m] long) to help support the wire. The easiest wire to handle for most garden jobs is 10 or 12 S.W.G.

To make the fence, clear the ground as for panel fences and erect a strainer at either end. To do this, drop the strainer into a tight hole, adjust it for height, and set it firmly upright by ramming down around it. Then position the prop along the line of the fence, one end stuck firmly in the ground, the other wedged against the post, and nail it in position. After fixing a building line between these two, erect the middle strainers and knock in the prick posts tight up against the line.

Finally, tack the strands of wire (the number will depend on the height of fence) to the posts and strainers with staples and working down from the top strain each strand in turn, driving the staples home when there is a good tension on the wire. For particularly long lengths of fence a small hand winch may be needed, but for most jobs pulling the wire firmly round the post will be sufficient.

Figure 97. Length of wire fence showing strainers and prick posts.

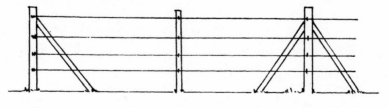

Screens

Building screens involves two considerations: first the design and size must be decided, and second, the strength of the screen must be considered. As far as possible the screen should be designed as an integral part of the piece of garden it stands in, and in this way its size and composition can be determined relatively easily.

The strength of the screen will depend on two factors: its height and whether or not it will be used to support climbing plants. With a lightweight screen up to 6 ft (1.8 m) high that will not be required to support plants, earth rammed firmly into the post holes will generally be sufficient to hold it. (For post lengths below ground see lapped panel fences, p. 136.) If, however, the screen is to be over 6 ft (1.8 m) or supporting plants, then it is better to use concrete in the holes and thicker posts. This particularly applies if the screen is to be made of materials that are not particularly robust such as panels or thin bamboo canes. (For screen designs see Figures 68–73.)

Conclusion

It is easy, when busy mixing ingredients or laying paths, to forget that we have been following the tenets and designs of Zen gardening; to overlook the particular magic that this concept lends to the gardens in Japan. This 'magic' springs, of course, not so much on how the garden looks at first sight, but from the way in which certain elements or points of design are used in the tradition of the Zen masters as aids along the route to enlightenment. Perhaps a story about Sen-no-Rikkyu, someone whose presence can be felt throughout this book, would illustrate this best.

Rikkyu had been asked to design a teahouse and garden, and the result at first disappointed the owner and his friends. The teahouse and the paths and garden around it fulfilled all expectations, but the magnificent view the garden commanded, one reason why the owner had chosen it, had been obscured by a line of densely planted cypress trees. What Rikkyu had done, which was not of course immediately obvious, was to make the view visible only when the observer was crouching down over the *tsukubai*, rinsing his hands and mouth, before entering the teahouse. In this position the view could be seen beneath the foliage; the full impact of the garden was withheld until the viewer was in a certain frame of mind, in this case the humble state of mind essential to appreciation of the tea ceremony. Alternatively, perceiving the view when in a crouching position may help to create, or initiate, the right state of mind for someone not already in it. It is not recorded, but all the same pretty certain, that once the owner of the garden realized the full sublety of Rikkyu's design, his doubts about it were removed.

We can be pretty sure of this because the gardens of Japan were used in the first place as vehicles for representing and expressing spiritual truths. This is illustrated by the close connection between the development of religion and that of garden design. This connection starts with the traditional native religions, where natural things were invested with spiritual power, and leads, through the symbolic use of gardens as a Buddhist heaven and the use of stones to represent Buddhas and the Buddha nature, to the use of rock arrangements and garden design to help people, priests in particular, to achieve religious enlightenment.

On a more general level, gardens provide the same kind of safety valve as many of the other aspects of the Zen influenced Japanese culture do, such as the tea ceremony, flower arranging and painting. They create a place and an atmosphere that can be used to recover, take a breath amidst the rush of life. Finally, it remains to point out that Zen gardens provide also sheer enjoyment, the pleasures of creating a garden, growing the plants, tending them and extending the design. Over and above themselves they have the universal appeal of gardens anywhere, the recreational side, the hobby, the centre for leisure hours, and I hope that this book will help find a larger place for them in the West.

APPENDIX 1

Waterfall Construction

The waterfall construction detailed in this Appendix is part of a garden laid out during the spring of 1978 at the Hakojuso old people's home in Osaka, Japan. I include this detailed description here to illustrate the way in which Japanese landscape gardeners, even today, approach their work with meticulous care and attention to detail, and the importance of this in the overall success of the garden. I hope too that it demonstrates the way in which traditional methods and ideas (as detailed in Chapters 1 and 3) are used in a contemporary setting, and the importance of these when landscaping in Japanese style.

On the last page of the illustration section are photographs of the waterfall taken during its construction. The whole arrangement looks somewhat new and bare, but in a couple of years, when the plants have grown, it will be surrounded in dense planting that will mould the components together. The fall group is made up of eighteen main stones, with the back built up with earth and smaller pebbles placed in the crevices between the big stones. Since it is impossible, until the actual stones arrive, to decide exactly what it will look like, the designer specified the main features of the fall (the pool at the top, the main curtain fall, the lower pool and the smooth falls into the water) and the group was built up to meet these requirements as closely as possible.

Before looking at the actual construction of the fall, two general points should be made about its design and the stones used. The side of the old people's home that overlooked the garden consisted of wide picture windows (that slid open in summer) so that people could sit in chairs and look at the garden. Thus, as can be seen in Figure 98, the waterfall had to be visible from a number of positions in the building and from the path leading in from the gate. It had,

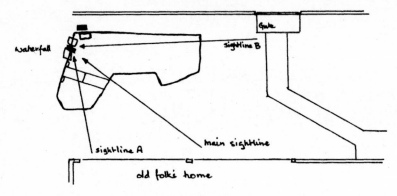

Figure 98.   Three sight lines govern the position of the waterfall stones.

therefore, to be a bold, open design where the stones and the falling water could easily be seen. To achieve this the designer settled on a wide curtain fall and lower pool where the water broke and splashed before carrying on to the pond. Working to these basic requirements the builders used the stones, positioning and re-positioning them many times, to create the desired effect. The stones themselves were brought from a river-bed site and contrast strongly with the bridge-supporting stones, lantern stone and the other pool-side stones which were quarried locally. The colours and smoothness of the river-bed stones not only make the waterfall look more natural, but also make it stand out more as the central feature of the pond.

CONSTRUCTION

1. Stones 1–6

As can be seen from Figure 99, the waterfall was to be situated across a corner of the pond in an area roughly 6 ft (1.8 m) wide, between the *yuki-mi-doro* stone on one side and the bridge-supporting stones on the other (these, and all the other pond edge stones were in position). The first stone, 1, to be positioned was important because it governed the way the fall actually entered the water. Since this was to be a smooth fall it had to have the right kind of surface and be positioned at just the right angle. Once the stone was chosen (Figure 100a), it took them about forty minutes to get its position right (Figure 100b).
Stone 2, chosen for its colours and beautiful stratification, was

142

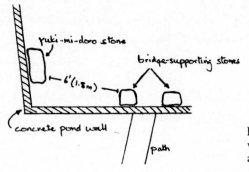

Figure 99.   Space available for the waterfall between *yuki-mi-doro* stone and the bridge-supporting stones.

a. Stone 1.

b. Stone 1 in position in front of concrete wall (section).

Figure 100a.   Choosing stone 1.   b.   Placing stone 1.

tried in various positions to the right of stone 1, and then, because they fitted together better, on its left. It had finally to be repositioned slightly so that stone 1 was visible along sight line A (see Figure 105), and its stratification lines were as horizontal as possible.

Stone 3 presented the first real problems. First, because its shape and size was governed by the space available between stone 1 and the. *yuki-mi-doro* stone; and second, because the shapes and bulk of stones 1 and 2 had to be balanced and contrasted. Basically, it could either be one tall, thin stone (Figure 101a) or built up of smaller ones (Figure 101b). A number of stones were tried for both methods but had to be rejected because they would not sit right with stone 1. One of these stones, however, had particularly eye-catching markings (whorls and twists in its stratification), and the design was altered slightly so that it could be used. This meant placing a small stone, 3, slightly forward of 1 and 2 so that the bigger one, 4, could be leant against it and the sloping edge of stone 1.

As can be seen in Figure 103, this stone 4, apart from being a feature in itself, complements the shorter, squatter appearance of

143

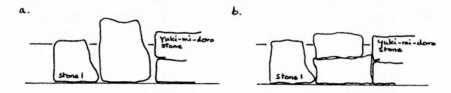

Figures 101a and b. Two possible ways of filling in the space for stone 3.

Figure 102. Earth built up behind the wall to support the back edge of stone 5.

stone 2 and creates a strong line of movement in the construction, that is ultimately carried on through stone 7 (see Figure 106).

With the final positioning of stone 4, the lowest level of the fall was complete and the stones were just above the level of the concrete wall. Before setting the next stones, therefore, earth and small stones had to be built up behind the wall to bring the level up. When this was complete, a stone had to be found that would create the lower pool into which the main curtain of water would fall. After a few attempts, a small flat stone, 5, was laid on the wall top, spanning the gap between stones 2 and 4, and just far enough forward to touch stone 1 (see Figures 102 and 103).

Attention was now turned to one of the most important stones of the whole construction: the stone that would create the curtain fall. This had to be a large rectangular stone with a smooth edge over which the water could fall. Once found, the stone, 6, was dropped on the built-up earth just behind stone 5 close enough for the falling water to splash onto stone 5 and just far enough back to allow a small pool to form at its base (Figure 104). When stone 6 was in position the actual path of the water down the fall was complete, falling over stone 6, over stone 5 and down stone 1 into the pond (see Figures 105a and b).

144

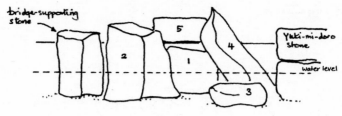

Figure 103.   Positioning of the first five stones.

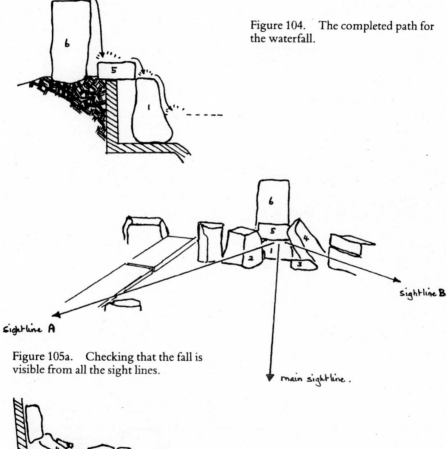

Figure 104.   The completed path for
the waterfall.

Figure 105a.   Checking that the fall is
visible from all the sight lines.

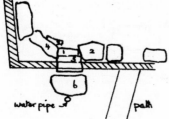

Figure 105b.   Positions of the first six
stones seen from above.

2. Stones 7–14

With the central part of the fall complete, another seven large stones were added to fill out the group and give it overall balance and cohesion. Stones 7 and 8 (see Figure 106) were difficult because they had to fit well with the sides of stone 6, while their shapes had to offset its solid square bulk. In addition to this, they had to form the sides of the group, bringing it together and focusing attention on the fall, and complement the lines of the lower stones. When these two had been found and positioned, the back wall (Figure 107) was built and the earth built right up behind and around stones 6, 7 and 8. While this was being done the 4 in (10 cm) inlet pipe for the water (see Figure 90a) was concreted in position up the back of stone 6, ready for when the header pool was constructed.

Stones 9, 10 and 11 (see Figure 106) were now used to fill in the group along the line of the lower pool and the earth was built up behind them. The final stones to be found were to form the header pool where the water would gather before falling in a curtain over the lip of stone 6. First a large stone, 12, was placed behind stone 6, chosen for its bulk and also because its roughly pointed top formed a natural peak for the whole group. Finally, stones 13 and 14 were dropped in to form the sides of the pool. (For a detailed diagram of a header pool see Figure 90b.)

Figure 106.   The completed waterfall.

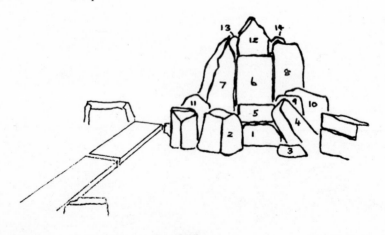

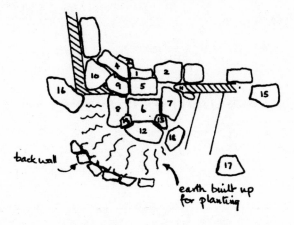

Figure 107.   The completed waterfall seen from above.

3. Stones 15–18

When the main group of stones had been constructed, it had now to be blended in with its surroundings and its bulk balanced out over a wider area. This was done by bringing the earth right round and behind the *yuki-mi-doro* stone on one side, and up to the bridge-supporting stones on the other. On these mounds four additional feature stones (15–18) were added (see Figure 107) to give the whole area an overall shape.

Finally, the joints of the waterfall stones were mortared up, pebbles placed in the pool, and small stones added at various points to create places where grasses and ferns could be planted.

In the last photograph the finished waterfall can be seen, before the water was turned on. At this stage of the work the pond and its edges are almost complete and planting of the main feature trees has begun.

APPENDIX 2

Plants and trees

The lists given in this Appendix are designed to give a general idea of the kinds of plants and trees that would be suitable for a Japanese-style garden. It is by no means exhaustive and should be used rather as a starting point for finding the plants that would best go with a particular layout. If, for example, a small layout has been planned then plants of the types given in category A would be the most suitable and so on.

Do remember, however, that the larger shrubs and some trees can grow to very considerable sizes and this must be allowed for in planning and positioning. If in doubt about the suitability of a particular shrub or tree consult someone at a garden centre or nursery.

A.
Small, dense shrubs and miniatures under 3 ft (90 cm)
B.
Medium-sized shrubs and small trees
C.
Large shrubs and trees for background planting or features
D.
Plants for ponds and pond edges. Bamboos.

A: SMALL, DENSE SHRUBS AND MINIATURES UNDER 3 FT

Buxus (boxwood) – dense, evergreen shrubs. Hardy and useful for low hedging. A number of varieties available.
Callicarpa – small, neat shrubs with beautiful colours in autumn. *C. dichotoma* and *japonica* are two compact varieties with pink flowers.
Cytisus austriacus – a dwarf broom with yellow flowers.

148

Daphne – beautiful, fragrant shrubs. A wide range of dwarf varieties are available.

Enkianthus – particularly beautiful flowers. *E. perulatus* is a dense variety from Japan. Masses of white flowers.

Ferns – all kinds useful in a number of places.

Hebe – evergreen with spring-to-autumn flowering; a number of varieties available.

Hydrangea – *H. arborescens* – a small, loose bush; *involucrata* – dwarf Japanese variety with blue and white flowers; *H. serrata* – miniature bush.

Hypericum – summer-to-autumn flowering. *H. calycinum* (dwarf) – evergreen with golden flowers. *H. elatum* – small, erect shrub.

Juniperus – a wide range of these evergreen shrubs are available, and they make an interesting feature. *H. compressa* is a dwarf variety.

Lespedeza – (bush clover) – *L. desmodium microphylla* (dwarf).

Potentilla – a wide range of very hardy dwarf-to-medium-sized shrubs. They give a useful spread and abundant flowers all summer.

Spiraea – easy to grow, graceful and hardy shrubs. *S. japonica* 'Little Princess' is a dwarf variety with compact growth and clusters of rose-crimson flowers.

B: MEDIUM-SIZED SHRUBS AND SMALL TREES

Aucuba – evergreen, shade-loving shrubs, whose dense, rounded shape make them ideal for back planting. *A. japonica* evergreen shrubs with dark, shining leaves and large red berries.

Azaleas – a wide range of these popular shrubs are available. They can be used to form many of the lower shrub groups illustrated in the layouts in this book.

Callicarpa – medium-sized shrubs with pleasant autumn foliage. *C. koreana* grows to 3 or 4 ft with pinkish flowers and mauve berries.

Corylopsis – very beautiful shrubs with a drooping habit. *C. glabrescens* and c. *spicata* are two wide-spreading, colourful shrubs suitable as the feature of a group.

Cotinus – (smoke trees) – summer-flowering with rich autumn colours. *C. coggyria foliis purpureis* purplish-red foliage which changes in autumn to a rich red.

Cotoneaster – versatile and hardy ornamental shrubs with abundant flowers and bright autumn colours. *C. rothchildianus* has a wide-spreading habit which makes it a useful filler for back planting.

Cryptomeria – globosa – dense, domed-shaped shrub which goes rust-red in winter.

Cytisus scoparius – the common broom with yellow flowers.

Enkiathus cernus rubens – Japanese species with brilliant autumn colours.

Hydrangea macrophylla – a wide range of these larger shrubs are available.

Juniperus pfitzerana – this evergreen grows with a low, spreading habit useful for a ground cover.

Lespedeza bicolor – a semierect plant with rose-purple flowers; *L. thunbergii* is autumn-flowering.

Mahonia – a number of these evergreen shrubs are available.

Nandina domestica – 'Sacred Bamboo' – a shrub found in nearly all Japanese gardens, particularly near water bowls.

Olearia hastii – evergreen shrub with abundant, fragrant white flowers in July–August.

Photinia glabra – evergreen with red fruits.

Spiraea cantoniensis – wide-spreading shrub with slender, arching branches and white flowers; *S. thunbergii* – dense with white flowers.

C: LARGE SHRUBS AND TREES FOR BACKGROUND PLANTING OR FEATURES

Large shrubs

Berberis – easy to grow, decorative shrubs, including *B. darwinii*, a large evergreen with abundant flowers.

Buddleia – flower July–September with a wide range of medium and large varieties available.

Camellia – hardy evergreens, including the *japonica* group, which flowers February–May.

Cotoneaster – brilliant autumn colours. Try *C. frigidus*, a small, spreading tree useful as a group feature.

Cytisus battandieri – tall, useful for back planting, yellow flowers in July.

Daphniphyllum – evergreens that grow well in shade. *D. macropodum* has good cover with small pink, fragrant flowers and large leaves.

Elaeagnos – good for wind breaks and back planting.

Euonymus japonica – large, dense shrubs.

Pittosporum – evergreen with good foliage. Try *P. tobira,* an excellent wall shrub with orange-blossom-scented flowers.

Rhododendrons – there are many varieties of this well-known shrub available which are useful for dense back planting.

Salia purpurea – willow. Forms a large bush with reddish-purple bark and graceful shape.

Viburnum – easy-to-grow woody shrubs. *V. farreri* has broad, round, scented, white flowers in winter.

Trees

Acer (maples) – hardy and easily grown, a feature of many gardens in Japan. *A. japonicum* is small and has very delicate leaves with spectacular autumn colours. *J. palmatum* (Japanese maple) – small trees with low, rounded shape.

Betula (birch) – graceful, delicate trees. *B. youngii* – small, dome, shaped weeping tree, particularly suited to pond edges.

Cercidiphyllum – good for autumn colours *C. japonica* is a small to medium-sized tree with smokey-pink autumn colours.

Crataegus – very hardy thorn trees, excellent for wind breaks and hedging.

Hamamelis (witch hazel) – hardy and attractive small trees.

Ilex (holly) – useful for hedging with a variety of shapes and colours available.

Juniperus chinensis – a popular ornamental tree.

Malus (crab apple) – flowering trees that make good features amidst shrubs. *M. echtermeyer* is low and wide-spreading with weeping branches.

Pinus (black pines) – evergreens are most suitable for training if kept small. *P. thunbergii* is the tree most commonly associated with Japanese gardens.

Prunus – pendula Rubra (cherry) lovely slender and weeping medium-sized tree.

Quercus myrsinifolia – compact evergreen useful for hedging.

Sorbus aucuparia (mountain ash) – small to medium tree suitable as a feature.

Thuja – evergreens with aromatic foliage. Small, conical trees excellent for dense planting. *I. rheingold* has rich deep-gold leaves.

Thujopis – similar to *Thuja* with broader, flatter branches. *I. dolabrata* is a small to medium tree, dense and conical with silver-backed leaves.

D: PLANTS FOR PONDS AND POND EDGES

Grasses:

Acorus gramineus – densely tufted evergreen with white-striped leaves.

Phalaris (gardener's garters) – excellent ground cover round ponds.

Water-lilies

Nymphaea froebeli – fragrant and medium-sized with crimson flowers.

Nymphaea laydekeri – useful for small ponds, rosy-lilac flowers and sweet scent.

Aquatic plants:

Acorus – *A. calamus* (sweet flag) – white, rose, gold leaves.

A. butomus umbellatus (flowering rush).

A. caltha (marsh marigolds).

Iris – *I. laerigata* – from Japan, with deep blue flowers.

I. 'Snow Drift' – large, pure-white flowers.

Rushes:

Scirpus albescens – colours change.

Scirpus tabernaemontani – white and green.

Typha – miniature rush for small pools.

Mosses: all kinds.

Bamboos:

Arundinaria – *A. hindsii* produces strong-growing, dense thickets (2.5–3.5 m.); easily grown.

A. marmorea, a low-growing (1–2 m.) plant with deep purples.

A. murieliae grows to 3.5 m. or more, producing elegant arching clumps, excellent for back planting.

Sasa:

Smaller than *Arundinarias*. Low and thicket-forming. *S. veitchii* has interesting colours throughout the winter.

Index